# THE POWER OF HUMAN SEXUAL FANTASY

—

*Effect over Sexual Orientation,*
*Culture and Crime*
-- Revision --

By
Alvah Buckmore, Jr.

# Dedication

I dedicate this book to my wife, Lolita.

ISBN-10; 1500534951
ISBN-13; 978-1-50053-495-0

# Table of Contents

# Preface

This edition of the "The Power of Human Sexual Fantasy: Effect over Sexual Orientation, Culture and Crime" is a revision of the first edition published on January 31, 2014 by the Strategic Book Publishing and Rights Company (ISBN: 978-1-62857-766-2).

Several significant changes were made with an increase of more than 3,000 words in this revision, namely an enlargement of certain issues I consider extremely important, plus an inclusion of Lewis Carroll, the pen name for Charles Lutwidge Dodgson of England (see page 128). He wrote "Alice's Adventures in Wonderland."

His entry into this Revision clearly fulfills our need to clarify the effect culture has over the interpretation of sexual orientation and crime. In our time, today, as an example, in the 20th and 21st centuries, anyone being in mere possession of child pornography can face criminal charges and receive the allegation of pedophilia. Upon a conviction in an American court of law, he could easily receive a sentence of 10 or more years in prison.

Yet, in the 19th century Victorian England at the time, taking pictures of children in the nude was acceptable under their standards. They did not even assign a sexual connotation to such activity. A study of his biography will reveal him to be a most interesting person who took high-quality photographs of children in the nude with their parent's permission while they watched him work in his studio.

So, when we read and study this subject of human sexual fantasy, and its effect over our sexual orientation, culture and crime, we must be completely objective and over-minded. It is a very complicated and difficult subject to handle properly.

Alvah Buckmore, Jr.,
September 2014

# Chapter One

## *Introduction*

As most of us know, or ought to know, there is a man's body and a man's brain, and a woman's body and a woman's brain. The body and the brain must match and have the same sex. With millions of components making up each body and each brain for a given sex, clearly millions of things can go wrong — and, unfortunately, frequently do.

To be entirely honest, most of us, including myself, lack the technical qualifications or knowledge to discuss, or even to identify, these millions of components and their interactions with each other to produce, finally, a working living human being — male or female. This subject is simply too complex for us — at least for the while!

So, we will confine ourselves to an examination and the developing hypothesis of the bonding mechanism that attracts us to the opposite sex; to each other; or to something else. That bonding mechanism is Human Sexual Fantasy, the mechanism that defines our sexual orientation. It is responsible for the way we develop and configure culture; controls our relationships with each other and can even lead us to crime and misery.

### The Bonding Mechanism —

The man, if his brain works correctly, will entertain a sexual fantasy of making love to a woman and that fantasy motivates, navigates and drives him into that direction.

The woman, on the other hand, if her brain works correctly, will entertain a sexual fantasy of making love to a man and, of course, that fantasy motivates, navigates and drives her into that direction.

It is this fantasy that bonds us to each other or to something else; if not to each other, then to something either innocuous or dangerous. Without it, we would not know what to do with the sexual tensions and pressures we feel every day. It is a navigational system with powerful motivational and driving attributes to direct and drive these tensions and pressures to the correct outlet — sexual intercourse and children. It can lead us to pleasure or pain or to something bizarre and dangerous. It can make our lives meaningful; provide us with direction or put us into a perpetual state of confusion for lack of direction and purposefulness.

The correct sexual fantasy for our sex, gender and species is the key to success.

There is nothing in American society, or in any other society, for that matter, with instructions or guidelines for us to know what to do beforehand or to provide us with medical treatment when something goes wrong, even if there is recognition of something wrong. All too often, however, there is no such recognition. Either we are in a state of denial or the problem is so far over our heads, we have no clue or recognition of an existing problem. There is nothing available to help us, either, even if we can intelligently talk about it; if everything works correctly, on the other hand, we will of course not need help. Everything is then instinctive and works automatically without any assistance from anyone.

Our American culture, as well as most cultures throughout the world, is full of biases, prejudices, "hang-ups" and a variety of other socio-psychiatric issues to make it very difficult, if not impossible, for most of us, to understand and to treat our condition if something should go wrong. On the most part, we cannot even talk about the subject.

In any community throughout the world, it is possible to walk down a street, in an inconspicuous manner, to observe people as they talk and interact with each other to perceive a "projection" of their sexual orientation or sexual preferences, or the kind of sexual fantasies they entertain — or even their

This illustration by Edouard-Henri Avril (1843-1928), a specialist in erotic art of the 19th century and early 20th century, clearly shows the relationship between sexual fantasy and masturbation. With modern video and computer technology unavailable at the time, he nevertheless demonstrated this relationship vividly with the image of a masturbating male while, with the use of a panel or fresco on the wall to his left — images of lesbianism, oral sex, sexual intercourse and sexual masochism. [Source: Wikipedia, the free encyclopedia]

lack of a sexual fantasy. With some exceptions, most of us "project" our fantasies and sexual preferences. Occasionally, we may find someone who deliberately either shutoffs his projections or projects a force field around his person to prevent people from recognizing his sexual preferences, such as his homosexuality and homosexual sexual fantasies with members of the same sex.

In other instances, there is simply nothing for him to project; he does not entertain a sexual fantasy. He subsequently leaves a blank on his person and, if not wearing the appropriate clothing to identify his sex and gender,  confuses his sex and gender identity to the casual observer. In most instances, he is aware of his problem and in turmoil.

In some instances, we may find a person projecting a particular sex and gender identity, but wearing the clothing and hairstyle, we associate with another sex and gender.

Sometimes, we may see a person transmitting images of gender confusion or even alternating between one gender and another, as if he were switching his *sexual orientation identity* from male to female and back, or something in between. His facial expressions will reveal enormous turmoil and intense frustration; for he has no clue, either. Nor will he receive help, recognition or sympathy with his problem. There is no help available for him anywhere; for our medical science is simply too primitive for the moment.

In many parts of the world, it is absolutely imperative for him to conceal his sexual orientation or preferences. Shutting off such projections, with some exceptions, will prevent most people from recognizing his sexual orientations and preferences; hence saving him from a lot of grief and hostility, even possibly the death penalty.

In some parts of the world, homosexuality is illegal and subject to the death penalty, though, on the most part, harmless to most people except to themselves, particularly when in a hostile environment.

In Nazi Germany, as an example, the SS put to death thousands of homosexual men and some women for no reason other than their homosexuality. They had done nothing wrong and had committed no crime. The SS even went to the extremes of burning books on the subject of homosexuality.

### One of the reactions by the Nazis --

With enough experience, it becomes possible to perceive and recognize we have a mental health crisis throughout the world and, on the most part, unrecognized as such. This mental health problem has been around for several centuries, at the very least, and most of us have not been smart enough to realize it. Actually, if we were to examine some

Nazis in Berlin (May 10, 1933) burned the books considered "Un-German," such as books on homosexuality, including the books looted from the library of Hirschfeld's "Institut für Sexualwissenschaft".
[Source: Wikipedia, the free encyclopedia]

ancient petroglyphs (rock engravings) in a variety of caves throughout the world, we will see evidence of this problem going back to nearly 40,000 years. It is not new!

Everywhere, millions of people are confused about themselves; their gender identity; or of their using a sexual fantasy driving them into dangerous waters -- such as pedophilia. They may have no ability to relate with either sex, or switch from one gender to another almost randomly with or without a corresponding sexual fantasy; or a secret knowledge they may have held for years since childhood: — The gender (sex) of their brain does not match the sex of their body. Also, some people may have the right gender for their brain to match the sex of their body, but entertain the wrong sexual fantasy for their gender and sex and, throughout the world, we have people, while the sex of their bodies stay constant, they switch their gender, from male to female and back, to suit their moods.

As we can well imagine, this creates enormous problems for them throughout every minute of their lives. It does not take much study on this subject, either, for us to realize we urgently need to understand it in much greater technical detail before we can do any good for anyone.

To make matters worse, our medical science and technology has nothing to offer in the way of a real knowledge or treatment of these issues, certainly nothing comparable to the recognition and treatment of -- say, diabetes, certain cancers, sleep apnea or a bipolar disorder.

We have a series of conflicting theories on these issues, and some of them exceedingly stupid; some of them dangerously irresponsible and spoken only in terms of hate and vulgarisms. Nor will it take much material to read before we will have begun to realize most of it as sheer nonsense to conceal our own ignorance and fears.

***

# Chapter Two

## *A hypothesis*

### Fantasy as a Navigational System —

If we were to examine our sexual fantasies, carefully and analytically, we would have to describe them as a complex computer program, next to the complexity of the human brain (a massively parallel processor). It probably has at least several million lines of instructions, with a set of mathematically intensive algorithms using relationships and toolsets we have yet to discover or develop. In fact, if I had to write out such a computer program, I would immediately find it way over my head. I would not even know where to begin!

One thing is certain, however. If we were to develop the knowledgebase to write out such a complex computer program to emulate Human Sexual Fantasy, we would immediately have a whole array of engineering applications all over the spectrum of human enterprise, plus the opportunity for the development of entirely new industries.

That would include navigational systems, automatic control systems, micro-management systems, environmental control systems on a micro-management level, weapon delivery systems, speech and image interpreters, language translators, etc. Only the limits of our imagination limit these applications.

An ability to write out a computer program to emulate Human Sexual Fantasy may also provide us with the impetus to develop the medical science, technology and industry to re-program our sexual orientation to match our gender and sex. We might call it Psychorientatis, a Dutch derivative, meaning, "To change [our] orientation."

## A Derivative of this Study --

A derivative from this thesis on human sexual fantasy, though outside the scope of this book, is the power of intellectual fantasy or daydreams.   Despite the fact its objective is obviously different than human sexual fantasy, its internal machinery, with its complex set of mathematically intensive algorithms and computer programs may differ only slightly in some of its crucial details.

Human sexual fantasy has the explicit purpose to bond us to each other for the purpose of procreation.  If it were not for this bonding mechanism, we would not know what to do with each other.

Likewise, intellectual fantasy works in a similar way. Only its purpose is different.  It motivates, navigates and drives us to better ourselves.   It is the mechanism responsible for human development, from the invention of the wheel to space exploration.  Each development started with a fantasy or daydream.  Else we would not have made any notable progress since the inception of our species of nearly 200,000 years ago, unlike the Neanderthal who had been around for at least 600,000 years and, during that time, made little or no progress to improve his life and standard of living, perhaps for the lack of an intellectual fantasy to drive him into development.

He interbred with Cro-Magnon man (European Early Modern Humans) and, it is believed, also with Homo sapiens; yet, still, he proved unable to progress beyond his initial stage of biological development.  The most he could do, judging from the evidence accumulated from paleoarcheological sites (the archaeology of deep time or the distant past), was to copy and use the tools made by Homo sapiens.   Unlike the Homo sapiens,   however,   he apparently could not daydream or entertain an intellectual fantasy; perhaps for this reason, he proved unable to make any technological progress for his kind or to compete with any species with such intellectual abilities.

***

# Chapter Three

## *Theories on the Origin of Sexual Orientation*

Below is a summation of several major theories dealing with the origin of sexual orientation, some of it serious and some of it foolish — since before 1864 to the present.

### The "Third Sex Theory"—

Karl Heinrich Ulrichs (b. August 28, 1825 in Aurich, Germany; d. July 14, 1895 in L'Aquila, Italy), is seen by the Homosexual Community as the pioneer of the modern gay rights movement. Starting off as a German lawyer, he published several pamphlets to declare a "man-male love" as inborn. He described homosexuality as a natural, normal and healthy expression of a "female soul in a male body" and called it "Uranians."*

### Bisexual Embryo —

In 1896, Magnus Hirschfeld (b. May 14, 1868 in Kolobrzeg, Poland; d. May 14, 1935 in Nice, France), a German physician, sexologist and an outspoken advocate for sexual

---

*Uranian** is a 19th-century term that referred to a person of a third sex—originally, someone with "a female psyche in a male body" who is sexually attracted to men, and later extended to cover homosexual gender variant females, and a number of other sexual types. It is believed to be an English adaptation of the German word, **Urning**, which was first published by activist Karl Heinrich Ulrichs (1825-95) in a series of five booklets (1864-65) which were collected under the title *Forschungen über das Räthsel der mannmännlichen Liebe* ("Research into the Riddle of Man-Male Love"). [Source: Wikipedia, the free encyclopedia]

Karl Heinrich Ulrichs (28 August 1825—14 July 1895) is seen today as the pioneer of the modern gay rights movement. [Source: Wikipedia, the free encyclopedia]

minorities published "Sappho and Socrates." He founded the Scientific Humanitarian Committee, perhaps "the first advocacy for homosexual and transgender rights."

Hirschfeld held the position that, in the embryos of both sexes, "there are rudimentary neural centers for attraction to both males and females." In most of the male fetuses, the sexual orientation toward women develops, while the sexual orientation or attraction to men loses ground, and then the opposite occurs for women. In the fetuses "destined" to become homosexual, on the other hand, the opposite develops. The male fetuses grow up with an attraction to other men and the female fetuses an attraction to other women.

Above is a photograph of the tomb of pioneering sexologist and homosexual rights advocate Dr. Magnus Hirschfeld (1868-1935) in the Caudade Cemetery in Nice, France. The headstone features a bronze bas-relief portrait of Hirschfeld in profile by German sculptor Arnold Zadikow (1884-1943). Gerard Koskovich, the author, took this photograph on a rainy day one day before the 75th anniversary of Hirschfeld's death.

*This file is licensed under the* Creative Commons Attribution. From Wikipedia, the free encyclopedia

He admitted he did not know the location of these centers; however, Hirschfeld believed, upon research and identification of its location, it will prove adults of each sex carries the "remnants" of his sexual orientation typical for the other sex. Staying in accord with the then current ideas about this corruption, he believed, the cause might lie with the parents' deteriorating "seeds on account of alcoholism, syphilis, and so forth." Perhaps, in recognition his own parents had led very good lives; he "... added rather lamely that homosexuals could also crop up in apparently healthy families," suggesting he really did not understand the cause

and effect relationships of homosexuality. Neither did
anyone else!

In 1903, he published Der Urnische Mensch ("The
Homosexual"). He did not believe there was a single male-
female taxonomy, categorization or hereditary program to
assign anyone to a given sex at birth. Rather, he held there
were a number of sex-related traits, including anatomy,
genital anatomy and the anatomy of other parts of the body —
the personality and sexual orientation — anyone of which we
could describe as being more male-like or more female-like.
Thus, he thought of sex as "multidimensional" and the male
and female attributes as abstractions.

He was a German physician working in Berlin, a sex
researcher and empiricists, a socialist, a Jew, and founder
of the world's first gay rights movement — the "Scientific-
Humanitarian Committee" (SHC). He was also Gay who
spent his life trying to understand his condition, the reason(s)
for it and, particularly, to legitimatize and hence decriminalize
it in Germany and the entire world. It was a crime in Germany
under Section 175 of the Penal Code; however, when Hitler
and the Nazis got in power in 1933, his application to
decriminalize Section 175 was set aside — principally due to
Hitler's incompetence and prejudices on the subject.

### The Theory of Constitutional
### Bisexuality and Immaturity —

It was Sigmund Freud (b. May 6, 1856 in Pribor, Czech
Republic; d. September 23, 1939 in London, England) who
wrote, in 1905, "Three Essays on the Theory of Sexuality."
He developed several sexual theories on the origins and
interpretations of homosexuality.

He believed homosexuality might have been the natural
outcome of normal development in some people, and found
it could occur in anyone with no previous indication of a
discrepancy or injury in his behavior. Nevertheless, he
did not view homosexuality as evidence or a symptom of

mental illness, by which he meant a symptom arising from emotional conflict, and viewed homosexuality as an uncomplicated expression of an inherent or inborn instinct beyond his control.

He called his belief or theory: -- "Constitutional Bisexuality." In every individual, he said, there was a certain facet or side of an active masculinity and a certain facet or side of passive femininity. He called them bisexual tendencies and declared them universal for humankind, but failed to consider the effects of culture and the genetic power relationship between men and woman forging such active and passive facets.

Sigmund Freud was an Austrian physician who started out in neurology but became known as the founding father of psychoanalysis. [Source: Wikipedia, the free encyclopedia]

Some people were encoded or programmed with a sexual orientation in preference to another sexual orientation, he thought; but said it differently from the way we would say it today.

Our traumatic life experiences, from our cultural and physical environment, would have definitely, he thought, an impact on our development and the way we express our natural instincts. See Chapter Eight, An Exception to Defective Code in the Fantasy-Making Machinery, page 108.

In normal circumstances, without a corresponding trauma to change the recipe, the ingredients that make up our instincts should determine our gender and it should be consistent with the sex of our body. In order words, the gender (sex) of our brain should match the sex of our body, and the sexual fantasies we entertain should match our brain and body for the correct sexual orientation (the author's interpretation of Freud).

Then, he added, a man should articulate the masculine natural instinct of his sex to obtain sexual satisfaction from women and, presumably, a woman should articulate the feminine natural instinct of her sex to obtain sexual satisfaction from men. That means a man should entertain a fantasy of sex with a woman and a woman should entertain a fantasy of sex with a man for them to be sexually compatible with each other.

Nevertheless, he believed adult heterosexuals preserve homosexual components or elements of homosexuality, but in a sublimated form. In other words, although a heterosexual man or woman may be strictly heterosexual in their behavior and sexual fantasies, there is an ingredient or programming code in our makeup that allows us to reverse this role if we were inclined to do so.

To Freud, adult homosexuality is an arrested development from childhood instincts preventing the development of a more mature heterosexuality (see Freud's Theory of Immaturity).

In a 1951 edition of the American Journal of Psychiatry, they published this from Freud:

> *"Homosexuality is assuredly no advantage, but it is nothing to be ashamed of, no vice, no degradation, it cannot be classified as an illness; we consider it to be a variation of the sexual function produced by a certain arrest of sexual development. Many highly respectable individuals of ancient and modern times have been homosexuals, several of the greatest men among them (Plato, Michelangelo, Leonardo da Vinci, etc.). It is a great injustice to persecute homosexuality as a crime, and cruelty too...."*

### The theory of "In-womb hormonal secretions"—

Eugen Steinach (b. January 28, 1861 in Hohenems, Austria; d. May 14, 1944) was a physiologist, hormone researcher and biology professor who became the Director of Vienna's Biological Institute of the Academy of Sciences in 1912.

**Eugen Steinach** (January 28, 1861 to May 14, 1944)
[Source: Wikipedia, the free encyclopedia]

In 1917, Eugen Steinach published his results on transplanted testes and ovaries in rats and guinea pigs in "Jahrbuch fur sextuelle Zwischenstufen" ("Yearbook of Sexual Intermediaries"). The results revealed that these glands secrete hormones into the bloodstream and affects the animals' physical development and sexual behavior. His argument was that these secretions were responsible for the sexual orientation ("*sexualization*") of the brain either as male or female. He suggested a person's sexual orientation ("*sexualization*") occurs early in life; however, he saw the most remarkable effects shortly after birth.

He held the attitude, in part influenced by Hirschfeld's biological theories; the testicular secretions in the homosexual male were deviant from the norm, leading to a female brain development instead of a male. He saw, he said, microscopic differences in the structure of the testis between homosexual and heterosexual men, and these differences were not in the sperm-forming cells but on the contrary, in the "interstitial"[1] cells. The "interstitial" cells are responsible for the secretion of testicular hormones.

It was in 1917 when he published an astounding report in the *Jahrbuch* describing the results of his transplanting a testicle from a heterosexual man into an "effeminate, passive homosexual man." He reported this operation completely "cured" him of the sexual orientation (attraction) to other men and, instead, developed perfectly normal heterosexual orientations.

Eventually, after some initial and subsequent successes, his procedure proved ineffective.

## Carl G. Jung's theory that parents influence sexual orientation —

Carl Jung (b. July 26, 1875 in Kesswil, Switzerland; d. June 6, 1961 in Zurich, Switzerland) was a Swiss psychotherapist and psychiatrist who founded Analytical Psychology. He developed the concepts of the extraverted and the introverted personality, and the archetypes and the collective unconscious in our culture.

In 1934, Carl Jung developed a theory that "every man carries within him the eternal image of [a] woman, not the image of this or that particular woman, but a definitive feminine image." He said this image is unconscious for us and of a primeval origin encoded in our DNA (though he did not use those words). It is an imprint or prototype of

---

[1]An **interstitial space** or interstice is an empty space or gap between spaces full of structure or matter. [Source: Wikipedia, the free encyclopedia]

Carl G. Jung in  1910 at the age of    35 [Source:
Wikipedia, the free encyclopedia]

all the inherited experiences of our women and of all the impressions ever made by woman in our DNA. Given that this image is unconscious, we are always unconsciously projecting it upon the person we love, and are one of the most important reasons for the passionate attraction or repugnance of people. ("The Development of Personality," 1934)

## The Theory of the Phobic Response —

Sándor Radó, (b. January 8, 1890 in Kisvarda, Hungary; d. May 14, 1972 in New York City), in 1940, rejected Sigmund Freud's theory of an inherent bisexuality; instead, he argued heterosexuality is inborn and that homosexuality is a phobic, hung-up or disturbed response to members of the other sex.

He was a distinguished Hungarian psychoanalyst of the second generation who moved to the United States in the 1930's.

He viewed homosexuality as a mental disorder and disagreed with Freud's hypotheses, a 19th century belief in *embryonic hermaphroditism*[2] (the idea that every embryo had the potential to become a man or a woman) and was the basis of Freud's "Constitutional Bisexuality."

Freud's hypothesis was wrong, he said. Sándor Radó argued that heterosexuality was the only non-pathological outcome of human sexual development. His views created a shift in his theory of pathology. For that reason, a number of analysts embarked on a claim they could "cure" homosexuality. Their work consisted of psychoanalysis to get at the root-cause for the same-sex attraction. They

---

[2] In biology, a **hermaphrodite** is an organism that has reproductive organs normally associated with both male and female sexes. Many taxonomic [science of classification of things or concepts] groups of animals, particularly invertebrates, do not have separate sexes. In these groups, hermaphroditism is a normal condition, enabling a form of sexual reproduction in which both partners can act as the female or male. For example, the great majority of pulmonate snails, opisthobranch snails and slugs are hermaphrodites. Hermaphroditism also found in some fish species and to a lesser degree in other vertebrates. Most plants are also hermaphrodites.

Sándor Radó (1890 to 1972) [Wikipedia, the free encyclopedia]

attempted to change the homosexual's attraction to the same sex. Physical treatments failed to work, however, such as bladder washing, rectal massage, castration and hypnosis.

### The Theory of "Normal Behavior"—

Evelyn Hooker (b. September 2, 1907 in North Platte, NE; d. November 18, 1996 in Santa Monica, CA) was an American psychologist. She is particularly important for her 1957 contribution entitled, "The Adjustment of the Male Overt Homosexual" in the Journal of Projective Techniques, Vol. 21, pp. 18-31. She conducted several undertakings dealing

 Evelyn Gentry Hooker, American psychologist September 2, 1907 to November 18, 1996 [Source: "The Mother of the Homosexual Movement — Evelyn Hooker PhD" in the July 16, 2007 edition of LITESITENEW.COM]

with the psychological tests of men who had identified themselves either as homosexual or as heterosexuals. She had asked people, experts on the subject, to identify the homosexuals from the heterosexuals and to measure their mental health. These experiments revealed no *"detectable difference between homosexual and heterosexual men in terms of mental adjustment."* Other researchers repeated the experiments revealing homosexuality not a mental disorder, as defined in DSM-I of 1952 (as a sociopathic personality disturbance).

She disputed the relationship between homosexuality and mental illness. This relationship, she said, was a twisted conclusion as a result of comparing homosexual men, with a history of treatment for mental illness, to heterosexual men without such a history. Her work successfully refuted the existence of the category of cultural heterosexism[3] when it demonstrated homosexuality as not developmentally inferior to heterosexuality.

It eventually led to the removal of homosexuality from the American Psychiatric Association's Diagnostic and Statistical Manual of Mental Disorders in the seventh printing of the DSM-II (1974).

*"Hooker,* [who was] *a professor of psychology at the University of California at Los Angeles for 30 years is credited in the medical and psychological community, and*

---

[3]*Heterosexism* is a system of attitudes, bias and discrimination in favor of opposite-sex sexuality and relationships suggesting heterosexuality as superior to the same-sex relationships.

*most especially amongst homosexual political activists, with establishing that there is no measurable psychological difference between heterosexual and homosexual men. Her work introduced and developed the idea that homosexuality, far from being a mental disorder, is merely a normal minority variant on human sexuality."* [Credit of quotation to Litesitenews.com]

## The Theory of Parental Relationships —

It was in 1962 that Irving Bieber (1909 - 1991), an American psychoanalyst, wrote "Homosexuality: a Psychoanalytic Study of Male Homosexuals," jointly with Harvey J. Dain, Paul R. Dince, Marvin G. Drellich, Henry G. Grand, Ralph R. Gundlach, Malvina W. Kremer, Alfred H. Rifkin, Cornelia B. Wilbur and Toby B. Bieber.

Dr. Bieber was a professor emeritus in the psychiatry department at New York Medical College in Valhalla, N.Y., and taught psychoanalysis. For 60 years, he researched and wrote on psychiatric issues. However, many in the Community have branded him for his troublesome view on homosexuality. He held the belief that homosexuality was a mental disorder that could be treated or prevented through psychotherapy — discredited by most researchers and analysts today — but not discredited by everyone.

He made the mistake of examining homosexuals already under psychiatric treatment and then comparing them to non-patient heterosexuals not under psychiatric treatment. It had almost the immediate effect of creating stereotypes later circulated by the media, and the effect of comparing "apples to oranges." Some writers, inspired by his work, continued to use the study today.

As an example, there is Joseph Nicolosi (b. January 21, 1947), an American clinical psychologist, founder and director of the Aquinas Psychological Clinic in Encino, California, and a founder and former president of the National Association for Research and Therapy of Homosexuality (NARTH).

Nicolosi advocates and practices "reparative therapy," a practice he claims will provide assistance to people who want to overcome, alleviate or ease their homosexual desires with heterosexual ones. (See his work entitled, "The Theory of Family and Cultural Factors")

Nicolosi believes homosexuality is frequently a condition of low self-esteem of his perceived gender-identity shortfalls. It is *"caused by an alienation from, and perceived rejection by, individuals of the subject's gender."*

Dr. Nicholas Cummings (b. July 25, 1924) says *"… since I was* [the] *APA president in 1979-80, the* [APA] *has been 'totally hijacked' by the homosexual/lesbian political lobby. It's incredible,…; having personally seen hundreds of people change the view that all homosexuality is hard-wired and same-sex attraction can never be changed is simply not supported by scientific evidence."* — Wikipedia, the free encyclopedia

## The Theory of Homosexuality is Biologically Derived —

In 1978, Frederick Whitam (b. February 7, 1933; d. July 10, 2009) was an American sociologist who studied homosexuality from a cross-cultural perspective.

His early works dealt with the sociology of religion before moving into the research of the universal patterns of male homosexuality in different cultures. He said, *"If you look at all societies, homosexuality occurs at the same rates with the same kinds of behavior. That suggests something biological going on. The biological evidence has been growing for 20 or more years."*

He also studied "Trans women."[4] In many cultures, he said, *"… these persons regard themselves as homosexuals and* [considered] *by more masculine homosexuals as a natural part of the homosexual world."* — Source: Wikipedia, the free encyclopedia.

---

[4] A **"Trans woman"** (sometimes **"Transwoman"**) is a male-to-female (MTF) transgender person with a female gender identity, perhaps a person with a man's body but a woman's brain.

Whitam's published books include "The Protestant Spanish Community in New York in 1960" and "Male Homosexuality in Four Societies: Brazil, Guatemala, the Philippines, and the United States in 1986." Robin Michele Mathy (b. July 21, 1957) co-authored it.

### The Theory of the "Inclusive Fitness"—

Edward Osborne "E. O." Wilson (b. June 10, 1929) is an American biologist, researcher (sociobiology, biodiversity), theorist (consilience, biophilia), naturalist (conservationist) and author. His biological specialty is myrmecology, the study of ants (considered as the world's leading authority).

In was in 1978 when he developed a theory of genetic tendency for homosexuality in certain humans he called "inclusive fitness."[5] He defined it as the *sum* of the individual's reproductive accomplishments and the reproductive accomplishment of other relatives carrying his genes. There are homosexual genes — not only existing in the individual who is homosexual — but also in all of his relatives. Homosexual people make their contribution to the family's survival by — not having children — but by making themselves accessible in the support of their families. Genes for a homosexual's sexual orientation increase in occurrence when they support the relatives who shared their gene pool and thus help to spread their genes through their relatives.

---

[5] To give an example of "inclusive fitness", Wikipedia provides the following: "The ground squirrel gives an alarm call to warn its local group of the presence of a predator. By emitting the alarm, it gives its own location away, putting itself in more danger. In the process, however, the squirrel protects its relatives within the local group (along with the rest of the group). Therefore, if protecting the other squirrels in the immediate area will lead to the passing on to more of the squirrel's own genes than the squirrel could leave by reproducing on its own, then natural selection will favor giving the alarm call, provided that a sufficient fraction of the shared genes include the gene(s) predisposing to the alarm call."

## The Theory of "Structural Brain Differences"—

Simon LeVay (b. August 28, 1943) is a British-American neuroscientist renowned for his studies about brain structures and sexual orientation.

In 1991, he wrote an article entitled, "A Difference in Hypothalamic Structure between Heterosexual and Homosexual Men," published in the Aug. 30 issue of Science magazine.

In this article, he reported a difference in average size between the third Interstitial Nucleus of the Anterior Hypothalamus (INAH3)[6] in the brains of heterosexual men and homosexual men:  INAH3 was more than twice as large in heterosexual men as in homosexual men. The INAH3 size of homosexual men was the same as that of women.

LeVay wrote the opinion: *"This finding indicates that INAH is dimorphic* [combining qualities of two kinds of individuals in one] *with sexual orientation, at least in men, and suggests that sexual orientation has a biological substrate* [surface on which a plant or animal lives]."

He added, *"It's important to stress what I didn't find. I did not prove that homosexuality is genetic, or find a genetic cause for being gay. I didn't show that gay men are born that way, the most common mistake people make in interpreting my work. Nor did I locate a gay center in the brain. The INAH3 is less likely to be the sole gay nucleus of the brain than a part of a chain of nuclei engaged in men and women's sexual behavior."*

Nancy Ordover wrote in her 2003 book, American Eugenics, that LeVay has been criticized for *"his small sample size and for compiling inadequate sexual histories."*

---

[6] INAH3 is the short form for the third interstitial nucleus of the anterior hypothalamus, and is the sexually dimorphic nucleus of humans. Homologues of the INAH3 have been observed taking a direct role in sexual behavior in rhesus monkeys, sheep and rats." [Source: Wikipedia, the free encyclopedia]

## The Theory of Virus and/or Bacteria Responsible for Homosexuality —

Paul Ewald[7] (no date of birth available) is an evolutionary biologist, specializing in the evolution of infectious diseases. Dr. Ewald has been working on a theory suggesting that many apparently noninfectious chronic diseases may have an infectious origin, including, perhaps, the origin of sexual orientation. He noted some mental illnesses might have infectious origin. The Streptococcus infection [*a genus of spherical Gram-positive bacteria*] can cause an obsessive-compulsive disorder in a straight line or due to a stimulated immune response. Bornavirus or a relative may cause schizophrenia. Depression is too common to be of a genetic origin, Ewald said, but it could have an infectious cause. Even homosexuality may have an infectious origin, he thinks, for it works contrary to the nature of our species and could not continue if it were part of a genetic program inside of us. *"Like many great ideas in biology, the idea implicating infectious causation in chronic diseases, though simple, has far-reaching implications. It is so simple and so significant, that one would think it would have been recognized by many and would be the starting point for any discussion on the causes of disease. Not yet."*[7]

*"It opens our eyes to many quite weird possibilities about disease that most medical scientists, tending to be unaware of current evolutionary thought, don't think of."* — Evolutionary biologist William D. Hamilton (b. August 1, 1936; d. March 7, 2000)

## The Theory of "Complex Traits and Multiple Causes"—

Dean Hamer (b. 1951) is an American geneticist, author and filmmaker known for his contributions to biotechnology and the prevention of AIDS. AIDS (Acquired Immune Deficiency

---

[7] **Ewald, Paul W**. (2002). Plague Time: The New Germ Theory of Disease. Page 56. (ISBN 0-385-72184-6)]

Syndrome) is the final stage of the HIV infection, a condition caused by the human immunodeficiency (the immune system's ability to fight infectious disease is compromised or destroyed) virus that gradually destroys the immune system and makes it harder for the body to fight infections.

Research on the genetics of human behavior included sexual orientation and spirituality.

In the August 6, *1999* edition of Science magazine (Vol. 285, p. 803a), he wrote, *"Sexual orientation is a complex trait that is probably shaped by many different factors, including multiple genes, biological, environmental, and sociocultural influences."*

In the 1990's, he began to study the role of genes in human behavior. In 1993, he published a thesis to suggest there could be genes to influence homosexuality in males, and offered some evidence one of these genes is associated with the Xq28 *marker* on the X chromosome. Two studies in the United States, but not a third in Canada, replicated his work.

He wrote several books and made several documentaries on a wide variety of topics.

Dean Hamer has published the following books dealing with this subject:

"The Science of Desire: The Search for the Gay Gene" and the "Biology of Behavior" (Simon and Schuster, 1994) ISBN 0-684-80446-8; "Living with Our Genes: Why They Matter More Than You Think" with Peter Copeland (Anchor, 1999) ISBN 0-385-48584-0; and "The God Gene: How Faith Is Hardwired into our Genes" (Doubleday, 2004) ISBN 0-385-50058-0.

## The Theory Sexual Orientation is Uncertain and Complex —

George Rice (date of birth unavailable) is the Professor of Neurology at the University of Western Ontario, Canada.

*"No one knows what causes heterosexuality, homosexuality or bisexuality* (in reference to a person's sexual orientation)."

*"Homosexuality was once thought to be the result of troubled family dynamics or faulty psychological development. Those assumptions are now understood to have been based on misinformation and prejudice. Currently there is a renewed interest in searching for biological etiologies* [the study of the cause or its origin] *for homosexuality. However, to date there are no replicated scientific studies supporting any specific biological etiology for homosexuality? Similarly, no specific psychosocial or family dynamic cause for homosexuality has been identified, including histories of childhood sexual abuse. Sexual abuse does not appear to be more prevalent in children who grow up to identify as gay, lesbian, or bisexual, than in children who identify as heterosexual."*[8]

It is Professor Rice's opinion the origin of anyone's sexual orientation is definitely uncertain and exceedingly complex. In 1999, he wrote in Science magazine on August 6, (Vol. 285, p. 803a), *"The basis of sexual orientation remains uncertain, but the Pathways involved can be expected to be complex. The controversies and methodological difficulties notwithstanding, the study of sexual orientation contain fascinating riddles, and further careful systematic study has the potential to reveal important insights about who we are."*

## The Theory of Multiple Causes —

Daryl J. Bem (b. June 10, 1938) is a social psychologist and professor emeritus at Cornell University. He originated the theory of self-perception of the attitude change, and carried out research on the phenomena of extra-sensory perception, group decision making, handwriting analysis, sexual orientation and personality theory and assessment.

In the August 6, 2000 edition of "Archives of Sexual Behavior " (Vol. 29, Issue 6, and Page 531 pl), he argued the *"Biological*

---

[8] **The American Psychiatric Association** wrote the above information in a May 2002 article titled *"Gay, Lesbian and Bisexual Fact Sheet,"* published on its website, Psych.org.

*variables such as genes or prenatal hormones do not code [program] for sexual orientation per se but for childhood temperaments [personality, character, disposition, spirit, etc.], such as aggression and activity levels. A child's temperaments predispose him or her to enjoy some activities more than other activities....Children who prefer sex-typical activities and same-sex playmates are referred to as gender conforming; children who prefer sex-atypical activities and opposite-sex playmates are referred to as gender nonconforming."*

*"To the extent biological factors such as the genotype [The genetic constitution of an individual organism], prenatal hormones, or brain neuroanatomy influence an individual's later sexual orientation, they do so only indirectly, by intervening earlier in the chain of events to influence a child's preference for sex-typical or sex-atypical activity and peer preferences — his or her gender conformity or nonconformity."*

## The Theory of Family and Cultural Factors —

Joseph Nicolosi (b. January 21, 1947) is an American clinical psychologist, founder and director of the Thomas Aquinas Psychological Clinic in Encino, California. He is also a founder and former president of the National Association for Research and Therapy of Homosexuality (NARTH). Look for him in The Theory of Parental Relationships and the effect of his work and conclusions by Irving Bieber.

Nicolosi has described his theories in "Reparative Therapy of Male Homosexuality: a New Clinical Approach" and three other books. Nicolosi proposes that homosexuality is often the product of a condition he describes as *gender-identity deficit* caused by an alienation from, and perceived rejection by, individuals of the subject's gender.

Joseph Nicolosi says on his website, *"… Homosexuality is almost certainly due to multiple factors and cannot be reduced solely to a faulty father-son relationship. Fathers of homosexual sons are usually also fathers of heterosexual sons — so the personality of the father is clearly not the sole cause of homosexuality. Other factors I have seen in the development of homosexuality include a hostile, feared older brother; a mother who is a very warm and attractive personality and proves more appealing to the boy than an emotionally removed father; a mother who is actively disdainful of masculinity; childhood seduction by another male (see page 108); peer labeling of the boy due to poor athletic ability or timidity; in recent years, cultural factors encouraging a confused and uncertain youngster into an embracing gay community; and in the boy himself, a particularly sensitive, relatively fragile, often passive disposition."*

## The Theory of Developmental Problems —

Traditional Values Coalition (TVC), in their description (2002-2003), says, "Traditional Values Coalition is the largest non-denominational, grassroots church lobby in America. Founded in 1980, by Rev. Louis P. Sheldon, Chairman, TVC has sought to empower people of faith through knowledge," and describes their mission as, *"With an emphasis on the restoration of the values needed to maintain strong, unified families, Traditional Values Coalition, focuses on such issues as religious liberties, marriage, the right to life, the homosexual agenda, pornography, family tax relief and education ... TVC believes America's strength is in her churches. Pastors and their churches are not barred by law from being involved in the making of public policy. Traditional Values Coalition provides a multitude of information for Christians and pastors, to equip them with the information they need to be educated on issues and on the representative form of government."*

They hold the following attitude on homosexuality: *"The most credible research to date on homosexuality — and research conducted years ago — demonstrates that no one is 'born gay.' The homosexual is suffering from a developmental problem, which frequently starts out in childhood as gender confusion, family dysfunction, or molestation ... There is hope for homosexuals through developing a relationship with Jesus Christ, through both religious and secular counseling programs, and through support groups that provide accountability for those struggling with same-sex attractions and self-destructive behaviors."*

Then, there is the nearly exact opposite conclusion ... or opinion.

### The Theory of "The intrauterine Hormonal Events"—

Vernon L. Quinsy (no biography available) is Professor of Psychology, Biology, and Psychiatry and Head of the Department of Psychology at Queen's University.

In 2003, he said of his article in the Annals of the New York Academy of Sciences (Vol. 989, pp. 105-117), *"People discover rather than choose their sexual interests. The process of discovery typically begins before the onset of puberty and is associated with an increase in the secretion of sex hormones from the adrenal glands. However, the determinants of the direction of sexual interest, in the sense of preferences for the same or opposite sex, are earlier. These preferences, although not manifest until much later in development, appear to be caused by the neural organizational effects of intrauterine hormonal events. Variations in these hormonal events likely have several causes and two of these appear to have been identified for males. One cause is genetic and the other involves the sensitization of the maternal immune system to some aspect of the male fetus. It is presently unclear how these two causes relate to each other. The most important question for future research is whether preferences for particular-aged partners and parts of the male courtship sequence share cause similar to those of erotic gender orientation."*

## The Theory of the "Transaction between Nature and Nurture"—

Matt Ridley (b. February 7, 1958), Matthew White Ridley, 5th Viscount Ridley, FRSL, FMedSci, DL, known commonly as Matt Ridley, is a British scientist, journalist, popular author and a member of the House of Lords.

In his book, "Nature v. Nurture; Genes, Experience, & What Makes Us Human" (Harper Collins Publishers, Inc., 2003), he says, *"Nature versus nurture has been declared everything from dead and finished to futile and wrong—a false dichotomy* [splitting a whole into exactly two non-overlapping parts]. *Everybody with an ounce of common sense knows that human beings are a product of a transaction between the two ... I believe human behavior has to be explained by both nature and nurture."* [Biology: The sum of environmental influences and conditions acting on an organism, such as nourishment, training and cultivation]

Ridley has written several science books including "The Red Queen" (1994), "Genome: the Autobiography of a Species in 23 Chapters" (1999) and "The Rational Optimist: How Prosperity Evolves" (2010).

"The Red Queen: Sex and the Evolution of Human Nature" is a popular science book by Matt Ridley exploring the evolutionary psychology of sexual selection.

His book argues we can understand very few characteristics of human nature apart from sex for the simple reason human nature is a consequence of evolution driven purposely by sex.

"Genome: the Autobiography of a Species in 23 Chapters" suggests the ways genes can affect human life; from our physiology to our diseases and behavior, and covers the history of genetics. This includes the theory of Mendelian inheritance, eugenics to improve the genetic composition of a population and then Francis and Crick to, perhaps, re-structure our DNA to improve Humankind and through nourishment, training and cultivation.

In "The Rational Optimist: How Prosperity Evolves," he reminded us that, over a period of nearly 10,000 years, there were less than 10 million people on the planet. Today, however, we have more than 6 billion people. Yet, most of them, perhaps as many as 99% of them are much better fed, better sheltered and better protected against disease than our ancestors of that period. In relation to our ancestors of that time, we are living "high on the hog."

Almost everything we need or want is improving — unevenly perhaps, as he suggested — throughout these last 10,000 years, but has actually accelerated over the last 200 years.

Everything from our calories, vitamins, our drinking and cooking water, machines, and our privacy has improved most significantly. Our means of transportation has improved most significantly, too, particularly in the last 100 years, and our ability to communicate with each other around the planet is nothing short of phenomenal.

*"Yet, people still cling to the belief that the future will be nothing but disastrous,"* he noted. Just look at some of the movies coming out in the theater and on television.

He is clearly optimistic with our future. If I understand him correctly, he feels there is no problem we cannot resolve. Sexual orientation is both a subject and problem we do not yet understand. However, whether homosexuality is a psychiatric disorder or a condition within normal limits, we still need to understand it in order to work out a solution, if it turns out to be a problem outside of normal limits.

### The Theory of Environmental, Cognitive and Biological Factors —

The American Psychiatric Association states, on their website (www.APA.org), *"There are numerous theories about the origins of a person's sexual orientation; most scientists today agree that sexual orientation is most likely the result of a complex interaction of environmental, cognitive  and biological factors. In most people, sexual orientation is shaped at an early age. There is also considerable recent evidence to suggest that biology, including genetic or inborn hormonal factors, play a significant role in a person's sexuality. In summary, it is important to recognize that there are probably many reasons for a person's sexual orientation and the reasons may be different for different people."*

Then, it asks, "Is Sexual Orientation a Choice? "

*"No, human beings can not choose to be either gay or straight. Sexual orientation emerges for most people in early adolescence without any prior sexual experience. Although we can choose whether to act on our feelings, psychologists do not consider sexual orientation to be a conscious choice that can be voluntarily changed."*

### The Theory "Genes pass down by material relatives —

Natalie Wolchover [she is on Facebook], a Staff Writer for the Life's Little Mysteries website, said that, when we consider that the male homosexual sexual orientation is sex with men, instead of women, it would automatically discourage sex with women. Therefore, men having sex with men would seem to prevent a homosexual man of genetically passing on to the next generation. Then, there is that logical question: *"why are there gay men at all?"*

As Natalie Wolchover    (http://blogs.scientificamerican. com/incubator/2012/05/02 /introducing-natalie-wolchover/) [also found in Facebook], to put it differently: *"why have gay man genes not driven themselves extinct?"* They are not having sex with members of the opposite sex!

Finally, new and ongoing research has answered the question. Studies by Andrea Camperio Ciani [b. Feb. 9, 1958 Florence, Italy] [http://ciani.socialpsychology.org/], of the University of Padova in Italy, plus others, discovered mothers and maternal aunts of gay men tend to have appreciably more children than the maternal relatives of straight men.

The same genetic factors that bring on homosexuality in males  also promote fecundity ( *a tendency of producing abundantly*) in their female relatives. Their female relatives pass on their homosexual genes in their future generations in spite of their lack of sex with the opposite sex.

Then, the question: *"How do females reproduce more successfully?"*

Camperio Ciani made a study of this phenomenon and came up with the following answer. It seems the mothers and aunts of homosexual men have an edge over the mothers and aunts of heterosexual men: -- These women are more prolific and display far fewer gynecological disorders or complications during their pregnancies. They are healthier, more extroverted, perhaps funnier, happier and more relaxed. Therefore, they seem to have less family problems and social anxieties.

In short, compared to other women, they attract the best heterosexual men allowing these women to produce bigger families and healthier children.

***

# Chapter Four

## *The Religions, their Interpretations and Treatment of Homosexuality*

### Pat Robertson Says Gay People Are Really Heterosexual —

In sharp contrast to the contemporary research conclusions and opinions by people who have studied homosexuality scientifically, and related subjects on a professional level, Pat Roberson has drawn a very different conclusion and opinion.

Pat Robertson has asked his lesbian, gay, bisexual and transgender followers to "come out" as straight people.

He has reported that thousands of homosexual men and women have said, *"Yes we want to follow Jesus, we're not happy with the lifestyle we're in and we want to have a better way."*

Robertson argued homosexual men and women are really not homosexual, technically speaking, but "confused" because of their childhood abuse or "chromosomal damage."

See Chapter Eight, "An Exception to Defective Code in the Fantasy-Making Machinery," Page 108. It may explain the reason for his interpretation of some of the homosexual behavior he may have observed in some of them.

*"A lot of people are into this homosexual thing because they've been abused by a parent, abused by a coach, abused by a sibling, abused by a friend.*

*"They're little boys and little girls and they don't know any better. And then they somehow think, 'Well, I must be gay.' They aren't. They are heterosexual and they just need to come out of that,"* he believes.

*"There are others, maybe they've got some chromosomal damage, that's different from heterosexuals. And that's of course what they claim in the homosexual movement. They say, 'Hey, you can't come out of this under any circumstances.'"*

36

## Religion and homosexuality —

This relationship between religion and homosexuality vary significantly throughout the world in both time and place. Contemporary doctrines of the world's major religions also vary a great deal from each other.

Among the various denominations with generally negative attitudes toward sexual orientations, other than a straight heterosexual orientation, there is a variety of different ways for them to articulate their negative attitudes. It can vary from discouraging homosexual activity, to explicitly forbidding homosexual practices among devotees, to vigorously opposing social acceptance of homosexuality — to murder.

Many of these religious doctrines argue it is the homosexual behavior, such as sex with a member of the same sex, which is sinful, wicked or a violation of God's law, rather than the state of being homosexual itself.

Several religious organizations, as well as several psychoanalytic businesses, exist to provide conversion therapy for any homosexual man or woman with the desire to convert to heterosexuality.

Nevertheless, within many of these religions, there are also people who view the sexual orientation of homosexuality with a favorable attitude, and many of them may even bless same-sex marriages and support LGBT rights. Throughout the world, there is a growing acceptance or tolerance of laws to support and protect LGBT rights in the United Nations.

Throughout history, many cultures and religions have accommodated, institutionalized, even respected, valued or honored same-sex love and sexuality.

There are mythologies and traditions around the world to support that above statement.

In one example, some Hindu denominations do not consider homosexuality a sin. The United Kingdom Hindu Council, an umbrella organization for all Hindus living in the United Kingdom, may have been one of the first major religious organizations to support LGBT rights with the official statement *"Hinduism does not condemn homosexuality"*.

Nevertheless, people who believe in their religion will

always look at both their sacred texts and traditions for their perceived proper interpretation and treatment of homosexuality.

## The Abrahamic religions —

The Abrahamic religions of Judaism, Christianity and Islam, have traditionally forbidden sodomy [*non-penile/vaginal cop-ulation-like act, such as oral or anal sex, or sex between a person and an animal*], and consider such behavior as sinful. Some denominations today, but again within   these Abrahamic religions, are more tolerant of homosexuality, such as Reform Judaism, the United Church of Christ and the Metropolitan Community Church.

Some Presbyterian and Anglican churches embrace members regardless of anyone's same-sex sexual practices, with some provinces permitting the ordination of homosexual clerics and the support of same-sex unions.

## Judaism —

The first five books of the Hebrew Bible, the Torah, is the crucial starting place for Jewish views on homosexuality. "*A man shall not lie with another man as he would with a woman; it is an abomination*" (Leviticus 18:22). As with many similar commandments, the death penalty is the punishment for intentional violation. Lately, in practice, rabbinic Judaism denies it now has the authority to implement the death penalties, though it did not deny any such authority much earlier.

Orthodox Judaism views homosexual acts as sinful, wicked, evil or immoral.

Conservative Judaism has been busy in a continuous study of homosexuality for almost 20 years. An assortment of

François Elluin, *Sodomites provoking the wrath of God*, from *Le pot* pourri *de Loth*, 1781 [Source: Wikipedia, the free encyclopedia]

Rabbis has presented a wide array of **responsa** [*consisting of a body of written decisions and rulings given by legal scholars in response to questions addressed to them*] for public contemplation.

Their official position is to welcome homosexual Jews into their synagogues and to fight against any discrimination. Reform Judaism and Reconstructionist Judaism in North America and Liberal Judaism in the United Kingdom look at homosexuality as normal as heterosexuality.

Progressive Jewish authorities believe traditional laws against homosexuality must change to reflect a new understanding of human sexuality.

## Christianity—

Throughout the world, Christian denominations have held a huge variety of beliefs on the subject of homosexuality and homosexual activity, from complete denunciation to complete acceptance. Most Christian denominations receive people attracted to the same sex, although they teach homosexual sex as sinful.

## Religious protest of homosexuality in San Francisco —

Some liberal Christians are supportive of homosexuals.

The United Church of Canada, the United Church of Christ, the Episcopal Church, the Presbyterian Church (U.S.A.), the Evangelical Lutheran Church in America and the Evangelical Lutheran Church in Canada do not consider homosexual sex sinful, wicked or evil, and some more liberal Christians feel more sympathetic toward homosexuality.

Particularly, the Metropolitan Community Church was founded to serve the Christian LGBT (Lesbians, Gay, Bisexual, and Transgender) community.

The United Church of Christ and the Alliance of Baptists also close their eyes to homosexual marriages;  however, some parts of the Anglican and Lutheran churches accept these unions.

There are openly homosexual clergies within the Anglican Communion, such as Gene Robinson and Mary Glasspool. There are also openly homosexual bishops in the U.S Episcopal Church, such as Eva Brunne in the Lutheran Church of Sweden.

Recent events in The Episcopal Church, concerning homosexuality, have brought serious ethical debates, with their corresponding tensions, within the Church of England and the worldwide Anglican churches.

Some passages in the Old Testament can lead us to the conclusion homosexuals should be subject to the death penalty; indeed, Fred Phelps and Jerry Falwell interpret AIDS (Acquired Immune Deficiency Syndrome) among homosexuals as punishment by God.

Theologians in the 20th century, such as Hans Küng, Karl Barth, John Robinson, Bishop David Jenkins, Jürgen Moltmann, Don Cupitt and Bishop Jack Spong confront traditional theological interpretations of the Bible.

They argued these passages have been mistranslated, taken out of context, or do not refer to the way we understand homosexuality today.

Based on scripture texts, many Protestant churches condemn homosexual relationships. Lying with another man is a sinful act, with no reference made to women lying with women. Such references almost always refer to male homosexuality while ignoring female homosexuality.

While the Catholics founded its view on a natural law argument augmented by scripture and Thomas Aquinas, the traditional conservative Protestant bases their interpretation on scripture alone, and perceives homosexual relationships as a hindrance to heterosexual relationships. They perceive some Biblical passages as commandments for only heterosexual marriages.

The Catholics, on the contrary, have provided accommodations for un-married people as priests, monks, nuns and single lay people for over a thousand years.

## The Catholic Church —

The Catholic Church demands that homosexuals, or anyone who is attracted to people of the same sex, as well as to anyone un-married to a member of the opposite sex, must practice chastity.

The Catholic Church does not consider a homosexual relationship as a representation of true marriage. A proper marriage, it teaches, is possible only when it works as a team and life-long commitment between a man and a woman.

In accordance with the Church's sexual ethics, homosexual relationships come to nothing because the male and female organs do not complement each other. Only their sexual orientations attract themselves to each other, not the complementarity of their bodies [*a state or system that involves complementary components*].

## Mormonism —

The Church of Jesus Christ of Latter-day Saints teaches us we should not sexually arouse ourselves or our desires outside of marriage (meaning: using sexual fantasy). That includes people with sexual fantasies and desires toward people of the same sex. We should overcome these thoughts and desires through self-control and reliance on the atonement of Jesus Christ (in the satisfaction knowing he had died for us). The Church teaches us marriage is always between a man and a woman, a team relationship — essential to God's eternal plan.

## Islam —

Every major Islamic school of thoughts condemns or rejects homosexuality. The religion of Islam considers homosexual desires as a natural temptation; however, a sexual relationship between two people of the same sex is a transgression of the function and purpose of sex. In the Hadith tradition

[Hadith: *important tools fo r understanding the Qur'an and in matters of jurisprudence*], Islamic teachings take for granted same-sex attraction, but praise sexual abstention (of the same sex) and in the Qur'an condemn a homosexual consummation.[9]

This dialogue on homosexuality in Islam deals primarily with sexual activities between men.

Sexual relationships between women, if looked upon as a problem, receive the same treatment as for adultery (sexual intercourse between a married person and someone other than their spouse). Some women had been executed for their sexual indiscretions with other women.

Abu Ja'far Muhammad ibn Jarir al-Tabari (a prominent and influential Persian scholar and historian) records an execution of a harem couple under Caliph al-Hadi, the head of state in a Caliphate and the ruler of the Islamic Ummah, an Islamic community ruled by the Shari'ah.

## Bahá'í Faith —

Bahá'í law confines acceptable sexual relations only between a man and a woman married to each other.

People who believe in the Bahá'í Faith must refrain from sex outside marriage.

Bahá'ís will not impose their moral standards on anyone who does not accept the Revelation of Bahá' u'lláh, tablets written by Bahá'u'lláh, the founder of the Bahá'í Faith (published in 1978).

While the Bahá'í Faith requires moral decency and respectability in their sexual behavior, or even when it has nothing to do with sex, the Bahá'i doctrine takes into consideration the reality of human weaknesses and imperfections to call for tolerance and kindness.

---

[9] The Marriage (Same Sex Couples) Bill introduced into the UK parliament in 2013 specifically excluded non-consummation as a ground for the annulment of a same-sex marriage. See: http://www.publications.parliament.uk/pa/bills/cbill/2012-2013/0126/2013126.

Likewise, in respect to homosexuality, the Bahá i' doctrine expects the same tolerance and kindness as they do with their friends and themselves.

## Indian religions —

Among all of the religions originating in India — including Hinduism, Buddhism, Jainism and Sikhism — their religious doctrines addressing homosexuality say very little clearly in comparison to the Abrahamic traditions. Their religious authorities articulate a variety of dissimilar opinions.

An influential figure of Sikhism, in 2005, denounced homosexual marriages and the practice of homosexuality.

Yet, many people in Sikhism do not oppose gay marriage.

## Hinduism —

Hinduism consists of assorted groups, such as Shaivism, Vaishnavism and Shrauta, accompanied by numerous customs.

Among a huge variety of practices and philosophies, Hinduism includes a broad range of laws and prescriptions of daily morality based on karma,[10] dharma,[11] and societal norms (*social standards or conventions*).

It is a categorization of distinct intellectual or philosophical viewpoints, instead of a rigid set of beliefs with a supreme governing body. The majority of Swamis[12] oppose homosexual relationships according to a 2004 survey. A much smaller minority supports such relationships, however.

---

[10] **Karma** is the concept of "action" or "deed", understood as that which causes the entire cycle of cause and effect that originated in ancient India and treated in the Hindu, Jain, Buddhist, Sikh and Taoism religions.

[11] **Dharma** is the Law that "upholds supports or maintains the regulatory order of the universe".

[12] A **Swami** is an ascetic or yogi who has been initiated into the religious monastic order or to a religious teacher, founded by Adi Shankara.

Ancient religious texts, such as the Vedas (*a large body of texts originating in ancient India*), often make reference to a third gender known as Hijra, [13] neither male nor female.

Some see it as an ancient similarity or equivalent to modern western lesbian, gay, bisexual, transgender or intersex identities (Essentially, "intersex identities" are males who dress and carry themselves as females). However, this third sex received very little respect as an exile class of people in ancient texts. Ancient Hindu law books, starting from the first century, categorize non-heterosexual sex as adulterated or unclean.

Hinduism has taken a wide variety of positions on homosexuality, everything from positive to neutral — to antagonism.

Hindus seldom openly talk about sex in Hindu society and the issues of LGBT, a taboo subject, particularly among the stalwartly religious.

Hinduism, since Vedic[14] times, acknowledges the existence of a *"third gender."* Texts, such as Manu Smriti and Sushruta Samhita, as well as several other Hindu texts, contend either some people are born with assorted male and female sexual orientations, or, they are, as a matter of normal biology, sexually sterile.

Even today, people of the *"third gender"* (Hijras) [13] live throughout India on the society's margins, and still make a living in prostitution or as beggars.

A variety of Hindu religious laws contain bans on homosexual activity. Some Hindu myths and legends speak sympathetically of lesbian relationships, while individuals with their third-gender identities were highly regarded by Hindu myths and legends.

---

[13] **Hijra** means physiological males who have feminine gender identity, adopt feminine gender roles, and wear women's clothing.
[14] The **Vedas** ("knowledge") are a large body of texts originating in ancient India. Composed in Vedic Sanskrit, the texts constitute the oldest layer of Sanskrit literature and the oldest scriptures of Hinduism

Historically, Hindu groups have had no uniformed or unified view or doctrine concerning the issue of homosexuality. Each group had its own distinctive doctrine.

On July 2012, Gopi Shankar,[15] a Gender activist and a student from The American College in Madurai, coined the regional terms for "*gender queer people*" in Tamil.

Gopi said there are more than "20 types of genders", such as Transwoman, Transmen, Androgynous, [16] Pangender[17] and Trigender.[18] Ancient India refers it as Trithiya prakirthi or Tritiya prakriti.

The language of English and Tamil (a Dravidian language spoken predominantly by Tamil people of South India and Northeast Sri Lanka) are the only two languages that have names for all the genders identified so far.

### Jainism —

Jainism is an Indian religion that has sat down a path of non-violence towards every living creature with the emphasis of spiritual independence and equality between all forms of life.

For the ordinary person, in the religion of Jainism, the only fitting path for sexual fulfillment and gratification is within marriage. Homosexuality leads to negative karma [see footnote 10] when we perform sex outside of a heterosexual marriage.

---

[15] So far, we have been unable to obtain any biographical information about him. (See: http://www.thehindu.com/news/cities/ Madurai/article3702689.ece; http://articles.timesof india.indiatimes.com/2012-07-30/madurai/32941100_1_gender-madurai-lgbt; or http:// articles.timesofindia.indiatimes.com/2013-06-04/madurai/39739581_1_genders-book-tamil-nadu)

[16] **Androgyne**, in terms of gender identity, is a person who does not fit neatly into the typical masculine or feminine gender roles of their society.

[17] **Pangender** people are those who do not wish to use the label of female or male as their gender. They think of themselves as "all genders."

[18] A **trigender** person, depending on his mood or situation at the moment, may shift from one gender to another.

Jain   author Duli Chandra Jain (b. November  26,  1881; d.   January   30,   1960),[19]   wrote   homosexuality   and transvestism (the practice of cross-dressing) *"stain one's thoughts and feelings"* as they involve sexual passion.

## Buddhism —

Buddhism is a religion native to the Indian subcontinent encompassing a variety of traditions, beliefs and practices principally based on teachings credited to Siddhartha Gautama, commonly recognized as the Buddha ("the Awakened One").

Gautama Buddha, also known as Siddhārtha Gautama, Shakyamuni, or simply the Buddha, was a wise person, philosopher or intellectual on whose teachings were responsible for founding Buddhism. His exact date of birth and death are in doubt. However, most historians have dated his lifetime roughly between 563 BCE and 483 BCE. Recent opinions, on the other hand, have dated his death between 486 BCE and 483 BCE or, with some historians, between 411 BCE and 400 BCE.

He lived and taught in the eastern part of the Indian subcontinent

The most widespread articulation of Buddhist ethics are the Five Precepts (the basic Buddhist code of ethics) and the Eightfold Path (one of the principal teachings of the Buddha), teaches a person should neither be emotionally involved nor hunger for sensual pleasure.

The third of the Five Precepts is *"to refrain from committing sexual misconduct."* But this *"sexual misconduct"* guideline or dogma is an imprecise term and, therefore, it allows for an interpretation reliant or dependent on the personality type and social customs of the believer.

---

[19] He was a writer, publisher, poet, editor, linguist and an intellectual giant in the field of Jainism.

Buddhism, in its most basic form, fails to define what is right and what is wrong in absolute terms for the untrained believer. As a result, whether homosexuality is acceptable or not for a layperson is not a religious question by many Buddhists.

Generally, many believers perceive Buddhism as distrustful of sensual enjoyment and sexuality in general. Traditionally, Buddhists perceive homosexual behavior and gender variance as obstacles to spiritual progress in most of their schools of religious thought and doctrine. As such, monks are required to abstain from all sexual activity and thus, in fact, the Vinaya (the first book of the Tripitaka, Sanskrit word meaning the "Three Baskets"[20]) expressly prohibits sexual intercourse.

They believe anal and oral sex, as well as vaginal intercourse, amounts to sexual intercourse, subsequently resulting in permanent exclusion from Sangha.[21]

An exception in the history of Buddhism arose in Japan, during the Edo period,[22] with the celebration of male homosexuality, or more specifically, love between young novices and older monks.

In the third of the Five Precepts of Buddhism, it says one is to refrain from sexual misconduct, an interpretation to include homosexuality. The Dalai Lama of Tibetan Buddhism interprets sexual misconduct to include all homosexual sex, amongst both Gays and Lesbians, as well as any other sex, excluding penis-vagina intercourse. This ban on sexual misconduct includes oral and anal sex, masturbation or any other form of sexual activity with the

---

[20] It is the traditional term in use by Buddhist to describe their various canons of scriptures. The expression, "The Three Baskets", originally referred to three receptacles containing the scrolls on which the Buddhist scriptures were originally preserved.

[21] It most commonly refers, in Buddhism, to the monastic community of ordained Buddhist monks or nuns.

[22] The period between 1603 and 1868 in the history of Japan, when Japanese society was under the rule of the Tokugawa shogunate and the country's 300 regional Daimyo.

hand. The only acceptable form of sex is for the biological purpose of procreation.

However, the Dalai Lama does support human rights for all sexual orientation in spite of his opposition to deviant sexual behavior.

In Thailand, there are traditional descriptions suggesting that homosexuality developed as a karmic[10] outcome of the violation of Buddhist proscriptions against heterosexual sexual misconduct. These descriptions describe homosexuality as a hereditary or inherited condition not alterable by anyone, at least not in the homosexual's lifetime. There have been appeals for compassion from the heterosexual community. Since homosexuality is hereditary, they feel, it is no one's fault if someone should have been born homosexual and, therefore, compassion is appropriate and proper for them.

Buddhist leaders in Thailand, however, have condemned homosexuality; monks accused of homosexual acts were described as kathoey[23] and banned from ordination.

In an article by the BBC on April 27, 2009, senior monk Phra Maha Wudhijaya Vajiramedh expressed great concern of the flamboyant behavior of gay and transgender novices, such as their wearing make-up and tights, or revealingly tight robes, carrying pink purses and having "effeminately shaped eyebrows." Phra Vajiramedhi acknowledged the difficulties of excluding them from the monkhood. Instead, he introduced Thailand and Buddhism's "good manners" program — a first for the country.

## Sikhism —

Sikhism has no doctrine or position on the subject of homosexuality; but in 2005, a Sikh religious authority described homosexuality as against the Sikh religion, the Sikh code of conduct and the laws of nature. He called on

---

[23] **Kathoey or katoey** is a Thai term that refers to a transgender or an effeminate gay male in Thailand.

Sikhs to support laws against homosexual marriages. Many Sikhs disagree with this view, however, to argue the Sikh Scriptures promote equality for everyone and does not condemn homosexuality.

## Zoroastrianism —

The Vendidad,[24] one of the later Zoroastrian texts composed in the Artificial Young Avestan[25] language, lacks a precise date.

The Vendidad, as a rule, endorses procreation: *"The man who has a wife is far above him who lives in continence; he who keeps a house is far above him who has none; he who has children is far above the childless man; he who has riches is far above him who has none."*

## Chinese religions —

Among the Taoic religions of East Asia, such as Taoism,[26] fervent homosexual expression is generally discouraged; it does not lead to human fulfillment.

## Confucianism —

Confucianism is basically a social and political philosophy paying little attention to human sexuality, whether homosexual or heterosexual.

---

[24] The **Vendidad** or **Videvdat** is a collection of texts within the greater compendium of the Avesta. However, unlike the other texts of the Avesta, the Vendidad is an ecclesiastical code, not a liturgical manual.

[25] **Avestan** is an East Iranian language known only from its use as the language of Zoroastrian scripture.

[26] **Taoism** is a philosophical and religious tradition that emphasizes living in harmony with the Tao. The term Tao means "way", "path" or "principle", and found in Chinese philosophies and religions other than Taoism. In Taoism, however, Tao denotes something that is both the source and the driving force behind everything that exists.—Wikipedia, the free encyclopedia.

However, Confucianism does put emphasis on male friendships while Louis Crompton[27] argued that the *"closeness of the master-disciple bond it fostered may have subtly facilitated homosexuality"*.

The Analects of Confucius[28] does not mention homosexuality. "Biting the bitter peel", a euphemism for homosexual relationships at the time, commonly meant anal sex and mentioned as a tradition by several individuals in the Classic of History[29] as well as the Spring and Autumn Annals[30]—both texts belonging to the Five Classics.[31]

## Taoism —

In the religion of Taoism, there is no official position on homosexuality, as the term describes a variety of contrasting religious traditions. In a similar way to Buddhism, Taoist schools sought throughout history a definitive definition of sexual misconduct.

As a result, some schools in their literature included homosexuality as one form of sexual misconduct. In Taoist history, homosexuality was certainly not unknown, such as during the Tang dynasty when Taoist nuns exchanged love poems.

As is true in most cultures, attitudes about homosexuality within Taoism often mirrored the values and sexual norms or the folkways and mores of the entire Chinese society at a given time.

---

[27] **Homosexuality and Civilization** by Louis Crompton, published by Harvard University Press. p. 221.

[28] **Analects of Confucius,** is the collection of sayings and ideas attributed to the Chinese philosopher Confucius and his contemporaries, traditionally believed to have been written by Confucius' followers. It is believed to have been written during the Warring States period (475 BC-221 BC).—*Wikipedia*, the free encyclopedia.

[29] The **Book of Documents** is one of the Five Classics and a compilation of speeches of major figures and records of events in ancient China.

[30] The *Spring and Autumn Annals* is the official chronicle of the State of Lu covering the period from 722 BCE to 481 BCE.

[31] The **Five Classics** are five ancient Chinese books used in Confucianism as the basis of studies.

## Homosexuality in China —

It is documented the existence of homosexuality in China has been found well into ancient times. During one study, before the introduction of the Western culture in the mid-19th century, the Chinese thought of homosexuality as a normal part of life.

Some historians have disputed that study, however. Many early Chinese emperors may have had homosexual relationships with men along with heterosexual relationships with women (probably for the explicit purpose of procreation). They may have been fulfilling their emotional and sexual needs through a combination of homosexual and heterosexual activity without necessarily being bisexual, or any other particular orientation — other than a heterosexual orientation.

Their culture, at the time, may have allowed men and, perhaps, women, to fulfill their sexual needs in a bisexual curriculum without their entertaining bisexual sexual fantasies, as is true with real bisexuals (fantasies with both sexes).

It was not until the 19th and 20th century did opposition to homosexuality develop, according to one study, and that was through the Westernization work of the late Qing Dynasty. The Qing Dynasty was the last imperial dynasty of China, ruling from 1644 to 1912, preceded by the Ming Dynasty and succeeded by the Republic of China from 1911 to 1949; then succeeded by the People's Republic of China (PRC) to the present.

There is an influential study by Robert Hans van Gulik (August 9, 1910—September 24, 1967) to argue the Mongol Yuan dynasty (1271-1368)[32] had launched an ascetic attitude to sexuality. He argued the classical Chinese were unable to articulate homosexuality in a clear and kindly manner. It may require further research to determine if these homophobic attitudes in Modern China were the results of Western influence earlier. Nonetheless, it is undeniable homosexual sodomy was banned in the People's Republic of China for

---

[32] The dynasty was one of the shortest-lived dynasties in the history of China, covering just a century.

Yuan Emperor Album Khubilai Kublai Khan, Genghis Khan's grandson and founder of the Yuan Dynasty c. 1260 shortly before his death February of 1294 by Aniko or Anige (1245—1306 CE) [Source: Wikipedia, the free encyclopedia]

almost half of the twentieth century until legalized in 1997. In 2001, the PRC then removed homosexuality from the official list of mental illnesses in China.

## Paganism —

*"Paganism is a broad group of indigenous and historical polytheistic religious traditions — primarily those of cultures known to the classical world."* — Wikipedia, the free encyclopedia

In a broader picture, it includes any non-Abrahamic folk ethnic religion.

For almost 100 years now, Paganism or Neopaganism[33] has been a collection of new religious movements attempting to revive historical pre-Abrahamic religion.

---

[33] A group of contemporary religious movements influenced by or claiming to be derived from the various historical pagan beliefs of pre-modern Europe. — Wikipedia, the free encyclopedia

Sexual deviant matter in pagan mythology deals with references of mythologies and religious accounts, and includes stories of romantic and sexual relationships between people of the same sex, or the heavenly measures resulting in the change of their sex (of the brain).

Some people have interpreted these myths as representative of Lesbian, Gay, Bisexual or Transgender manifestations but within the framework or background of their contemporary concepts of sex and their sexual pastime.

Many mythologies attribute homosexuality and sexual variance as proof of a god or other supernatural intervention, including myths of gods teaching people about homosexual practices, or stories explaining the reason a person identifies himself as a sex (of his brain) opposite of the sex of his body.

Western mythologies, a long time ago, have recognized Lesbian, Gay, Bisexual or Transgender themes, a subject under passionate study but perhaps not truly scientifically. The attention given to gender studies (sexual characteristics and sexual categorizations) and queer theory focused on the mismatch between our physical sex and our sexual desire (a sexual orientation controlled by our fantasies), to non-Western traditional mythical collections.

As a symbol for sacred or mythical experiences, myths often include homosexuality, bisexuality or transgenderism. Devdutt Pattanaik[34] writes that myths "capture the collective unconsciousness of a people." They manifest our subconscious beliefs about variant sexualities at odds with more repressive social mores.

## Wicca —

Wicca is a modern-day pagan and witchcraft religion. Developed in England during the first half of the 20th

---

[34] **Dr. Devdutt Pattanaik** (born December 11, 1970—present) is an Indian physician turned leadership consultant, mythologist and author whose works focus largely on the areas of myth and mythology.

century, Gerald Gardner[35] (b. June 13, 1884; d. February 12, 1964) introduced Wicca to the public in 1954. He was a retired British civil servant.

His material drew upon an assorted collection of ancient pagan and 20th century irrefutable embellishments for its theological structure and ritual practice.

The Wiccan Charge of the Goddess,[36] one of the most famous texts in Neopaganism, states in the words of the Goddess, *"All acts of love and pleasure are my rituals"*. In traditional forms of Wicca, such as Gardnerian and Alexandrian Wicca, magic is performed between a man and a woman, and the "Great Rite" is a form of sex magic that includes either ritual sexual intercourse performed between a Priest and a Priestess to represent the God and Goddess, or a ritual symbolic representation of sexual intercourse between a man and woman.

Nevertheless, this usually does not exclude homosexuals or magic between homosexual couples. Usually, these initiations take place between a man and a woman, as most Wicca groups require. Any ritual sexual acts, however, whether actual or symbolic, shall be between two consenting adults — usually lovers.

### Satanism —

Satanism, in the LaVeyan Satanism, simply referred as Satanism among most of the adherents, is a tradition founded

---

[35] **Gerald Brosseau Gardner**, known by the craft name **Scire**, was an English Wiccan, as well as an author and an amateur anthropologist and archaeologist. He was instrumental in bringing the Contemporary Pagan religion of Wicca to public attention, writing some of its definitive religious texts and founding the tradition of Gardnerian Wicca. --Wikipedia, the free encyclopedia.

[36] It is a traditional inspirational text often used in the Neopaganism religion of Wicca. It is usually spoken by the High Priestess after the ritual of Drawing down the Moon. The Charge is the promise of the Goddess (embodied by the High Priestess) to all witches that she will teach and guide them. It has been called "perhaps the most important single theological document in the neo-Pagan movement." -- Wikipedia the free encyclopedia.

in 1966 by Anton LaVey (b. April 11, 1930; d. October 29, 1997).[37]

He based his philosophy on individualism, Epicureanism[38] and an "eye for an eye" morality open to all forms of sexual expression, which does not preclude homosexuality.

Satanism, in its Spiritual traditions, is also open to all varieties of sexual expression, including homosexuality, heterosexuality and bisexuality.

## Unitarian Universalism —

The Unitarian Universalist Association supports the freedom to marry anyone. It compares itself and its resistance to such constraints as to the same resistance of the abolition of slavery, women's suffrage and the end of anti-miscegenation laws.[39]

Several congregations have carried out a succession of organizational, procedural and practical steps well known as a "Welcoming Congregation", with a systematic program to accept and integrate Gays, Lesbians, Bisexual and Transgender members into their Church.

Unitarian Universalism ministers readily perform same-sex unions and same-sex marriages when legal and, even when not legal — as a form of civil protest.

The Unitarian Universalists, on June 29, 1984, became the first major church to accept religious blessings on homosexual

---

[37] **Anton Szandor LaVey**, born Howard Stanton Levey, was an American author, occultist and musician. He was the founder of the Church of Satan as well as the author of The Satanic Bible and the founder of LaVeyan Satanism, a synthesized system of his understanding of human nature and the insights of philosophers who advocated materialism and individualism, for which he claimed no supernatural or theistic inspiration.—Wikipedia, the free encyclopedia.

[38] **Epicureanism** is a system of philosophy based upon the teachings of Epicurus, founded around 307 BC. Epicurus was an atomic materialist, following in the steps of Democritus. His materialism led him to a general attack on superstition and divine intervention. — Wikipedia, the free encyclopedia.

[39] **Anti-miscegenation laws** that enforced racial segregation at the level of marriage and intimate relationships by criminalizing interracial marriage and sometimes sex between members of different races.

unions in the United States. Universalism largely accepts a theological belief every person and all creatures on Earth have a relationship to a god or to the divine and, upon his death, will be or must be prepared to accept a god.

Unitarian Universalists have been working hard to make homosexual marriages legal throughout the United States on the national level.

Gays and Lesbians are frequently ordained as ministers, and a number of them have become legally married to their partners.

Arlington Street Church (Boston, Massachusetts), on May 2004, was the location of the first state-sanctioned homosexual marriage in the United States. The official stance of the UUA is for the legalization of homosexual marriages.

## Queer religions —

We associate opposition to homosexual marriages and LGBT rights with conservative religious views. The American Family Association,[40] as well as other religious groups, have boycotted corporation policies supporting the LGBT community.

In conservative Islamic nations, as a good example, there are laws prohibiting homosexual behavior. Their interpretation of Sharia Law[41] on male homosexuality provides the death penalty on anyone caught at it. A human rights organization, such as the Amnesty International, has

---

[40] **The American Family Association** (AFA) is a United States non-profit organization that promotes fundamentalist Christian values. It opposes same-sex marriage, pornography and abortion. Founded in 1977 by Donald Wildmon, he calls it the National Federation for Decency with its headquarters in Tupelo, Mississippi. — Wikipedia, the free encyclopedia.
[41] **Sharia** is the moral code and religious law of Islam. Sharia deals with many topics addressed by secular law, including crime, politics, and economics, as well as personal matters such as sexual intercourse, hygiene, diet, prayer, *and* fasting. Though interpretations of Sharia vary between cultures, in its strictest definition it is considered the infallible law of God — as opposed to the human interpretation of the laws." — Wikipedia, the free encyclopedia.

condemned it as a violation of human rights and by the writers of the Yogyakarta principles.[42]

In the year of 2009, with finally the signature of the United States, every European secular state and all western nations, signed the proposed United Nation's declaration of human rights for the LGBT community. There are now a total of sixty-seven signatures.

However, the Muslim nations signed an opposition statement by 57 of its member states; most of them in Africa and Asia.

Sixty-eight of the total 192 countries have not yet signed.


## Islamic Religious Opposition —

In most Islamic countries, pursuant to Sharia law, homosexuality is a crime; and homosexuals and homosexual intercourse officially carries the death penalty in Saudi Arabia, Iran, Mauritania, Nigeria, Sudan and Yemen. They treat them as criminals.

That was also true in Afghanistan under the Taliban until the United States invaded Afghanistan to destroy al Qaida, founded by Osama bin Laden in Peshawar, Pakistan, and supported by the Taliban. To get at al Qaida, it was first necessary to destroy the Taliban.

In the United Arab Emirates, the legal state of affairs is ambiguous.

In some Islamic countries, homosexuality is punishable with jail time, fines or corporal punishment, such as in Bahrain, Qatar, Algeria and the Maldives. In other countries, with a Muslim majority, such as in Jordan, Indonesia or Mali, there is  no law explicitly prohibiting homosexuality. In Egypt,

---

[42] It ... "is a set of principles relating to sexual orientation and gender identity, intended to apply international human rights law standards to address the  abuse of the human rights of lesbian, gay, bisexual, and transgender (LGBT) people and issues of intersexuality". — Wikipedia, the free encyclopedia.

however, general public morality laws will prosecute homosexual men for openly practicing homosexuality. Conversely, homosexuality has been legal in Turkey for decades.

In Oman, the Xanith,[43] born as men but behave as if they were women, occupy a role in society that allows them to have sex with men as long as they accept the female role and receive the phallus (an erect penis).

The maximum punishment for homosexuality in Saudi Arabia is public execution; however, the government will use other forms of punishment — such as fines, jail time, and beatings — unless it feels the homosexual community has chosen to challenge their authority by engaging in LGBT social movements.

Iran has perhaps executed the largest number of its citizens for homosexuality. Since the 1979 Islamic revolution in Iran, they have executed more than 4,000 people for homosexual activity.

Homosexuality went from a capital crime, punishable with death, to one punishable with fines and prison after the fall of the Taliban in Afghanistan.

The Human Rights Watch and Amnesty International, as well as most international human rights organizations, condemn laws making adult homosexual relationships a crime.

Muslim nations stubbornly maintain such laws are necessary to preserve their Islamic code of morality and virtue, but without a thought given to the human or psychological or, particularly, the biological mechanism responsible for homosexuality; nor the legal, civil and human rights issues. Of all of the nations with a Muslim majority, only Lebanon has an organization trying to legalize homosexuality.

---

[43] **Xanith** is roughly equivalent to the word "faggot" in American English.

## The United Nations on the LGBT issues —

Human rights for LGBT (Lesbians, Gay, Bisexual and Transgender) at the United Nations focus mainly on making resolutions in the General Assembly and the United Nations Human Rights Council.

In the General Assembly, there is a proposed resolution supporting LGBT rights initially submitted in its original form by French/Dutch representatives in 2008. The European Union, in support of this resolution, remains open for more signatures. Ninety-four countries signed it so far.

In the United Nations Human Rights Council, there is another resolution to support LGBT rights by South Africa. This resolution passed in 2011.

From 1945 to December 2008, the United Nations had not discussed the equality of sexual orientations or gender identities until a Dutch/French delegation initiated a European Union-backed statement before the United Nations General Assembly.

The statement, originally designed to be a resolution, provoked an Arab League-backed statement opposing it. Both statements remain open for signature; however, the United Nations General Assembly has officially adopted none of the two.

This proposed declaration of equal human rights included a condemnation of violence, harassment, discrimination, exclusion, stigmatization and prejudice based on sexual orientation or gender identity, which undermines personal integrity and dignity.

There is also a provision condemning executions, torture, arbitrary arrest and the deprivation of economic, social and cultural rights.

The Declaration received praise for its breakthrough toward human rights. It overcame the previous prohibitions or restrictions against speaking out against LGBT abuses.

South Africa initiated a resolution in the United Nations Human Rights Council, on June 17, 2011, requesting the United Nations High Commissioner for Human Rights to provide a report describing the situation of LGBT citizens throughout the world, and to implement the Vienna Declaration and Program of Action.[44]

This resolution passed 23 to 19 with three abstentions: -- Burkina Faso, Zambia and China. It was the first such resolution and welcomed as "historic."

***

---

44 The **Vienna Declaration and Programme of Action**, also known as VDPA, is a human rights declaration adopted by consensus at the World Conference on Human Rights on 25 June 1993 in Vienna, Austria. The United Nations High Commissioner for Human Rights was created by this Declaration endorsed by General Assembly Resolution 48/121.

# Chapter Five

## *The Credibility of Psychiatry and the American Judiciary System*

In 1952, the first edition of the American Psychiatric Association's Diagnostic and Statistical Manual of Mental Disorders (DMS-I) classified homosexuality as a mental disorder, in which Sándor Radó was a significant influence; but the American Psychiatric Association removed this classification in 1973 under intense political pressure by gay rights activists. A protest by gay rights activists began in 1970 when the APA held its convention in San Francisco. They disrupted the conference with shouts and ridicule of any psychiatrist who described or interpreted homosexuality as a mental disorder.

At the 1971 conference sponsored by the American Psychiatric Association, Frank Kameny (May 21, 1925 -- October 11, 2011),[45] working with the Gay Liberation Front,[46] grabbed the microphone and yelled, *"Psychiatry is the enemy incarnate. Psychiatry has waged a relentless war of extermination against us. You may take this as a declaration of war against you."*

His activism occurred in the context of a much bigger storm against psychiatry, starting originally in the 1960s challenging the legitimacy, technical competence and integrity of psychiatric diagnosis -- and psychiatry itself.

---

[45] **Franklin Edward (Frank) Kameny** was "one of the most significant figures" in the American gay rights movement.

[46] **Gay Liberation Front** (GLF) was the name of several Gay liberation groups, one of the first formed in New York City in 1969, immediately after the Stonewall riots on June 28, 1969 in New York City, when the local police clashed with gay demonstrators.

Physician Johann Christian Reil coined the word "Psychiatry" in 1808 [Source: Wikipedia, the free encyclopedia] *This file licensed under the* Creative Commons Attribution.

With research data from   Alfred Kinsey (June 23, 1894   — August  25,  1956)[47] and  Evelyn  Hooker (September 2, 1907 -November 18, 1996),[48] the seventh printing of the DSM-II, in 1974, no longer listed homosexuality as a mental disorder and instead replaced it with the category of "sexual *orientation disturbance*".

In retrospect, when we look at the history of psychiatry and psychoanalysis, over a period of nearly 200 years, there is nothing short of bewilderment it took so long for a revolt of this systematic fraud and charlatanry. It was a German physician, Johann Christian Reil (February 20, 1759 to November 22, 1813), who coined the word "Psychiatry" in 1808, to mean the *"medical treatment of the soul"* out of recognition of such a need for a new science.

Over these many years, however, psychiatry has developed into more than a *"medical treatment of the soul"*, but both a science devoted to the study, diagnosis, treatment   and

---

[47]**Alfred Charles Kinsey** was an American biologist, professor of entomology and zoology, and sexologist who in 1947 founded the Institute for Sex Research at Indiana University.
[48]**Evelyn Hooker** (née Gentry), was an American psychologist most notable for her 1957 paper "The Adjustment of the Male Overt Homosexual"

prevention of mental disorders, and an intellectual assault weapon against the individual.

It has grown into a dangerous science, pseudoscience and weapon system — all at the same time — depending on the government(s) and the individual(s) using it. It is dangerous!

## In the Former Soviet Union —

In the former Soviet Union, as one example, the State used psychiatry to discredit dissidents and people who did not necessarily oppose or disagree with the ideology of Communism, but who held a slightly different opinion or interpretation from the mainstream thoughts on a given subject, or someone with "too many opinions." They held them in "psychiatric" institutions subject to "medical experiments," such as electric shock treatment or, perhaps, a partial removal of the brain with the belief it was responsible for the "bad thoughts." With many of these dissidents, the State gave them dangerous "psychotropic medication" with little thought given to the repercussions of the side effects.

They destroyed tens of thousands of lives in this way; basically a transparent attempt to maintain control and to hold onto to their powerbase. Opinions different than their own had the effect of eroding their powerbase, as they perceived it; hence, it was imperative to either destroy or to suppress people with such "dangerous" opinions.

Andrei Vladimirovich Snezhnevsky    (May 20, 1904 -- July 12, 1987) was a Soviet psychiatrist noted for his expansive diagnostic criterion for schizophrenia, another footstep allowing the State to stamp political dissidents as "*sluggishly progressing schizophrenics*" in order to legally justify their long-term imprisonments.

For a long time, the West condemned Snezhnevsky as a prime example of the political abuse of psychiatry in the Soviet Union. They charged him with the development of a system of diagnosis the Soviet state could bend for political purposes. He himself diagnosed or was involved in several prominent dissident cases, such as the biologist Zhores Medvedev (1925 to present) and the mathematician Leonid Plyushch

(1939 to present).

The psychiatrist, Marina Voikhanskaya (you will find her on Facebook), has accused Snezhnevsky of debasing Russian psychiatry to a *"semi-amateur level and single doctrine about schizophrenia"*, in which alcoholic psychoses and alcoholism is considered schizophrenia; congenial idiocy in the children of alcoholics is considered premature schizophrenia; and dissent is considered schizophrenia with delusions of reform.

The Special Committee on the Political Abuse of Psychiatry, in 1980, established by the Royal College of Psychiatrists in 1978 (the main professional organization of psychiatrists in the United Kingdom), accused Snezhnevsky of taking part in this pattern of psychiatric conspiracy and abuse. As a Corresponding Fellow of the Royal College of Psychiatrists, they invited him to attend the Court of Electors in order to address criticisms he was responsible for the compulsory incarceration of the celebrated dissident and Mathematician, Leonid Plyushch.

Snezhnevsky, consequently, had chosen to resign his Fellowship.

From the available data found in the archives of the International Association on the Political Use of Psychiatry, there is evidence the Soviet state imprisoned thousands of dissenters for political reasons.

### In the United States —

In the United States, for more than 100 years, thousands of people were prisoners in similar institutions and, once there, ignored for the rest of their lives unless they were fortunate enough to have a friend or relative who cared enough to rescue them from this kind of hell.

For at least the last 60 years, the United States Armed Forces have used psychiatry, psychotropic medication and psychiatric institutionalization (illegal imprisonment) to conceal crime among members of its leadership. If a serviceman were to see crime in his chain-of-command, or someone thought he might have seen something, or something he would see if he were to stay long enough, and his command did not want him to see it, it was not uncommon — if not a standard procedure — to place him into a psychiatric institution under heavy medication for a few months or a little longer before releasing him for home. He would then arrive home with an elaborate certified history of psychiatric illness in his medical records, and they would certify these records existed prior to his entry into the Armed Forces.

If his Primary MOS (Military Occupation Specialty) had required a secret security clearance, all references of that security clearance in his records may disappear.

His actual rank and grade may disappear on his discharge papers listing him with a lower rank and grade. Typically, these records would certify a history of schizophrenia, usually of the paranoid type. It would go into elaborate detail describing his childhood life and all of his difficulties of growing up into adulthood. It may include descriptions of his use of drugs and alcohol; problems with his family and schools and anything else the resident psychiatrist could imagine. Some times, there would be two or more people, working from an outline provided to them by his Commanding Officer or someone else in his command, to make it look as if a team of psychiatrists had conducted a most comprehensive psychiatric examination revealing schizophrenia and other psychiatric issues.

These documents would have all of the proper and appropriate stamps and certificates of legitimacy and, without an extensive criminal investigation outside of these documents, there would be no way to prove otherwise.

These documents would include a certificate to certify a panel of three psychiatrists had independently examined the diagnosis by the staff psychiatrist and found his diagnosis and all of the dots and dashes on his documents correct and proper.

While still at this institution, with some exceptions,

he would find all of the doctors, nurses and psychiatric technicians in agreement with the staff psychiatrist. Almost all of them, when the opportunity arose, will tell him it is "obvious" he is seriously mentally ill and therefore would require years of intensive psychiatric treatment and medication.

Then, once home and after receiving his discharge papers, which may partially contradict the medical records, he will receive a letter from his local Veterans Administration facility requesting an appointment to re-examine him for a re-evaluation of his medical condition(s).

At that point, once he will have arrived for his appointment, he would find an exact copy of as many as a hundred pages or more of documents falsely certifying a history of psychiatric illness going back prior to his entry into the Service (almost impossible, particularly if he had been issued a security clearance).

Interestingly, this psychiatric conspiracy ends at the Veterans Administration. The psychiatrist, charged with the responsibility to re-examine and to re-evaluate him will almost immediately perceive fraud, or the heavy contradiction between the material in his medical records and his behavior. Though far from perfect as a science, psychiatry is perfect enough for a trained psychiatrist to differentiate psychosis, such as the Schizophrenia, from a non-psychotic.

They see and work with psychotic personalities almost every day; so, it is easy for them to tell the difference between Schizophrenic personalities of the paranoid type from the non-Schizophrenic personalities of the paranoid type. Such people might as well have green skin with purple dots. It is not only obvious to the trained eye but also quite conspicuous!

This psychiatrist would write out a report of his observations and subsequent diagnosis and, as anyone might think, such a contradictory diagnosis should immediately bring forth a criminal investigation. But it does not! The report simply goes into the patient's files along with hundreds of other similar files in the VA's databases. It seems the top executive officers of the Veterans Administration, all the way to Washington, D.C., have been aware of these psychiatric conspiracies in the United States Armed Forces for years, possibly before the start of the Second World War, but have done nothing about it. Even most of our political leadership is aware of this problem and have done nothing about it.

The false psychiatric material stays in the veteran's files for everyone, with the correct password and qualifications, to read every word.

This creates an interesting and bizarre side effect. A nurse, who must have access to at least part of the veteran's file, sees the false diagnosis or diagnostic label on the front page of his records; accepts it on face-value and then proceeds to interpret the veteran's behavior within the framework of what he thinks he knows about psychiatry.

If the veteran's diagnosis says, "Schizophrenia of the paranoid type," the nurse may write down the following: "*Patient with history of Schizophrenia of the paranoid type has a temperature of 96.8° F with a blood pressure of...*"

If his visit is of a more serious nature, then the diagnosis in his medical files will include a test results modulated by the nurse's interpretation of the diagnosis in the veteran's file. The nurse may even attempt to perform a psychiatric diagnosis of his own, though not a psychiatrist or qualified to do so, to complement the original diagnosis with the following pretentious nonsense: "*The patient, with a history of Schizophrenia of the paranoid type, has shown features of serious paranoia today with clear tangentality*", suggesting the patient talked incoherently and did not make much sense in his paranoiac ramblings. Even when crystal-clear and precise, the nurse may perceive otherwise.

The nurse is trying to sound brilliantly perceptive in psychiatry and to make him look superior to his patients before his supervisor. It is an ego trip — and he gets away with it!

Then, in sharp contrast to this fraud and pretentiousness, a doctor or general practitioner, with a doctorate in medical science, but not psychiatry, may easily perceive the contradictions. If unaware of these psychiatric conspiracies originally, he may or may not say anything to his patient, but reports his suspicions to his colleagues later in the day, who may admit to knowledge of the U.S. Armed Forces' misuse of psychiatry. Nothing will become of it, however.

If the veteran were to file an application for a life insurance policy, he would have to sign a document to authorize the insurance company to access his military medical records and, in addition to the false psychiatric material, they will see the various derogatory comments by the nurses and doctors. Very likely, they will then decline the policy.

Going to American courts to expose this kind of conspiracy will prove difficult and, more likely, impossible. The federal government has jurisdiction over this kind of controversy with the Armed Forces. That means the veteran would have to file a civil complaint in the clerk's office of the local U.S. District Court. Filing a criminal complaint with the Attorney General of the United States is impossible, and doing the same before the appropriate military non-judicial remedial board will get him nowhere, either. They are criminal organizations.

Even if they were to believe the veteran's story, very few attorneys will handle such a controversy; hence, the veteran will have to represent himself as a pro se litigant. After writing out the Original Complaint, he would file his complaint in the clerk's office.

As long as he does everything correctly, and fills out the appropriate documents, he will have no difficulty with the clerks, unlike the state clerks who play games with pro se litigants of finding fault with every detail before processing the application.

However, once the U.S. Marshall's office delivers the summons and complaint to the Attorney General's office, he will then run into the games they play with pro se litigants. They will typically file an illegal motion to dismiss the case without legal justification with a series of nonsensical arguments, including the citation of case precedence that either do not exist or exit but support different or even the exact opposite opinion.

In time, the clerk's office will send an order for the pro se litigant to appear before the federal judge to hear his case. Once in court, the defense attorney, an Assistant Attorney General of the United States, will stand up before the judge for anywhere from 30 to 90 seconds, typically.

His arguments will be brief and always sheer nonsense. He will deny everything and all liability, knowledge or accountability. He may even suggest that the veteran is obviously incompetent or seriously mentally ill who may require further psychiatric treatment and medication. Then, he will sit down with no further comments or arguments.

His arguments will always contain little or no substance; nor will he meet the substance of any averment he denies, a legal requirement under the Federal Rules of Practice and Procedure. The judge will sit down on his bench and say nothing, but knowing full well these arguments violate law. They are not legal arguments in an American court of law.

However, once the veteran stands up to argue his case, the judge may suddenly change his facial expressions to express anger, contempt and impatience with the veteran. He has no time to listen to such nonsense and may literally scream at the veteran in open court to call him paranoid and incompetent, suggesting he would have had no problem if he had hired an attorney, knowing very well that was probably impossible for him.

Or, he may play the opposite role. He may listen patiently and talk respectfully to the veteran, giving the impression of integrity and fairness with a desire to resolve the controversy honestly.

A few days later, an order comes in from the judge dismissing the complaint with the same nonsensical arguments heard by the Assistant Attorney General. Of course, this is illegal and reveals an obvious collusion between the defense attorney and the judge.

It happens all of the time with the United States Government as the defendant. There is almost never a level playing field regardless of the nature of the controversy. When dealing with the abuse of psychiatry, however, we will find it almost infinitely more difficult.

Controversies of homosexuality and other forms of sexual deviations, with arguments of civil rights, justice and equality, would lead nowhere except under very special circumstances. It would take a team of dedicated and committed attorneys even to get to first base — with either this or most controversies with the United States. A lone non-attorney will have no chance. Our courts have never learned to handle such controversies with non-attorneys!

If the veteran were to appeal before the Appellate Division (Court of Appeal), he would run into the same problem.

If he should appeal before the Supreme Court of the United States, the Court will typically refuse to hear the case without a hearing. Every year, there are thousands of cases heard and dismissed in this fashion, most of them nothing to do with psychiatry or homosexuality, of course.

In time, if he were to live long enough to accumulate enough experience with courts, clerks, magistrates, judges and security systems, he might eventually discover collusion almost always develops between the courts and the defense attorneys when the plaintiff represents himself. He almost never has a level playing field. Depending on the severity of the controversy and the political connections of the defendants, even if he should come up with enough money to pay the retaining fee for an attorney, he may still find collusion between his attorney, the judge and the defense attorney(s).

They may actually communicate with each other almost immediately after the commencement of the case to work out a strategy to defeat him, and this collusion will continue all the way to the Appellate Division and, finally, to the Supreme Court. Do not expect honesty by anyone in today's courts, certainly not consistently — except by a quirk. That will happen once in a while!

Still, with some exceptions, this collapse of the conspiracy will not necessarily resolve the problem and indeed, may continue with new judges and clerks. Judges and clerks, who may have had nothing to do with the original conspiracy, may now participate in a continuing conspiracy with or without a formal agreement between them. They can be that stupid and dishonest, sometimes with nothing to gain from it and principally motivated by a feeling of belonging to the "Club."

Of course, there are exceptions. This becomes obvious, during a particularly ugly controversy of conspiracies among judicial members of the courts coming out of the woodwork; a single judge disqualifies himself and, perhaps, followed by other judges.

That would mean those judges want nothing to do with such criminal activity. Their only course of action is to get off and stay away from the case. Either they cannot effectively fight the wrong they perceive or lack the courage to reveal it to the appropriate agency.

In one notable instance in the summer of 1988, there was a similar case in which I, challenging the legality of false material in my military medical records at a local VA facility, found the Chief Justice, Warren Burger, of the Supreme Court of the United States, actively obstructing me. He attempted to intimidate me through the Clerk's office. Every time I sent my petition to the Court, the Clerk's office returned it with no reason given to me. In one instance, someone affixed a big "NO" on the front cover of the petition, obviously another attempt at intimidation.

In my Petition for a Writ of Certiorari, accompanied with 513 pages of legal documents in nine Appendices, through a procedural rule in the Rules of Practice and Procedure allowing me to bypass the Clerk's office for direct delivery to the Chief Justice, I discovered the Chief Justice was the culprit. Obviously, the Chief Justice did not want to hear the case. Though he resigned under political pressure, after I successfully wrote and published a letter in the local newspaper, it did not resolve the problem. My military records remain uncorrected and no one faced prosecution for his crimes.

Every year, thousands of people run into the same problem in their desperate attempt to resolve serious legal problems when unable to secure the services of an attorney, either due to the nature of their controversy or to the lack of funds, and every year almost all of them dismissed without a lawful hearing. Each time, the courts pretend to conduct such a lawful hearing, but with the same outcome pre-determined beforehand between the judge(s) and the defendant United States.

Again, there is never a level playing field. At every level in our judiciary system, from the lowest court to the highest court, with every step he takes to resolve his problem, his problem will actually get larger as the conspiracy between the courts and the defense grows bigger through a greater increase in the number of participates. These participants will participate in a conspiracy through the informal agreement, meaning they will have made no formal agreement to participate in a conspiracy and indeed may not even personally know each other. They are that stupid!

We can call this phenomenon the "Exponential Effect." It means that, with every successive attempt to resolve his problem, it gets exponentially larger with no end in sight.

Then, there is the phenomenon we call the "Good O'Boys' Network." It may be another psychiatric disorder, a condition in which two or more people work so closely together, they prove unable to separate the bond between them long enough to examine an issue outside of their relationship, such as a criminal complaint against one of them.

In this kind of working relationship, a complaint against one is a complaint against all of them, and the only time a complaint works is when the respondent falls out of good grace with the "Good O'Boys' Network."

In this kind of situation, regardless of the nature of the controversy, nothing works properly and no one does his job. Then, every once in awhile, someone does something right and all hell breaks lose. Careers go down the drain.

People resign without a word of the true explanation in the newspapers. Some people commit suicide and, again, the true reason is not to be found in the newspapers. Local obituaries may describe him as a great man of integrity; a giant in his field, while ignoring his true character as a corrupt judge, clerk magistrate or attorney, etc., who accepted bribes, kickbacks and participated in criminal conspiracies. Everything is forgotten, including the people he destroyed.

Other times, after all hearings, conferences, etc. are over and the final adjudications come in denying the validity of the original complaint, all of the defendants — without a word of explanation — will resign with no hint of their criminal involvement described in the newspapers, either, although many of the news reporters will know the truth. Our American news media is dishonest, ideologically motivated and driven and cowardly when it comes to the exposure of corrupt judges and a dysfunctional judiciary system.

In the United States — certainly as well as elsewhere — an individual person, with or without an attorney, particularly if representing himself, has no realistic chance of resolving such problems in an American court of law.

To be successful, it takes an enormous effort and monetary resources, in a coordinated team of men and women working together for a single goal, to make even the smallest contribution, particularly in areas of great controversy, such as human sexuality, gun control, the abuse of psychiatry, medical science and racism.

In these controversies, although most people know little or nothing about them, including human sexuality, almost everyone has a strong opinion, usually an opinion formulated from the nonsense traveling through the Grapevine Circuits. Under those circumstances, it is very hard to communicate with such people, including members of our news media and our political representatives. Just to gain access to them can be a challenge.

As is true with any field of great controversy, we will find it difficult to get at the truth.

\*\*\*

# Chapter Six

## *A Brief History of American Psychiatry Wrestling With the Problems of Categories and Classifications of Mental Disorders*

### Diagnostic and Statistical Manual of Mental Disorders (DSM) —

The American Psychiatric Association (APA) publishes the Diagnostic and Statistical Manual of Mental Disorders (DSM) and has the explicit purpose to provide a standard language and criterion for the category and classification of mental disorders. Ideally, it serves to help the medical field to use the same language and tools to communicate with each other when dealing with a complex diagnosis.

The United States uses DSM extensively and, to some degree, also in use throughout most of the world. Clinicians, researchers, psychiatric drug regulation agencies, health insurance companies, pharmaceutical companies, our judiciary system and even political and administrative policy makers use it.

Presently, the version in use, published on May 18, 2013, is the DSM-V or DSM-5.

This Manual evolved from consensus, psychiatric hospital statistics and, also, from a United States Army manual. Since 1952, there has been a periodic increase reported in the number of mental disorders and, at times, some of them, after a considerable amount of discussion and arguments, removed when no longer thought not to be mental disorders, or when too dangerous to describe it as such.

We routinely use The International Statistical Classification of Diseases (ICD) and Related Health Problems, published by the

World Health Organization (WHO), as another manual listing the criterion for mental disorders. It is the official diagnostic system for mental disorders in the United States, and extensively used in Europe and various parts of the world. Nomenclature used in the DSM corresponds with the nomenclature in use by the ICD. However, sometimes this is not true, and not all of the nomenclatures match each other due to the lack of coordination between the two publications.

There has been some admiration and praise for the standardization of psychiatric diagnostic categories and criterion in the DSM — understandably. We need it!

There has also been much serious controversy and criticism with the arguments the DSM reflects an unscientific and subjective system of analysis. That is also true!

Almost constantly, we have unending issues with references to the soundness and the trustworthiness of these diagnostic categories. DSM, their critics argue, relies on superficial symptoms and the use of man-made divisions between "normal" and "not normal" behavior based on cultural bias, prejudices and, quite plainly, ideology and/or to maintain hold onto power (such as in the former Soviet Union), or to conceal crime (such as in the United States) and many other places elsewhere.

The original motivation and driving force for developing a a classification of mental disorders in the United States, then again, was an urgent need for collecting statistical information in order to more fully understand the subject. That was a perfectly valid and an honest reason, of course

In 1840, there was an official attempt to use a single category of "idiocy/insanity," but there was not enough data or accumulated experience to break down psychiatric illnesses into greater detail or to develop nomenclature — a very important objective.

A Committee on Statistics, in 1917, now known as the American Psychiatric Association (APA), working with the National Commission on Mental Hygiene (NCMH), established a guideline for mental hospitals. They called it the "Statistical Manual for the Use of Institutions for the Insane." It contained 22 diagnoses.

APA subsequently revised this several times over the years. They, along with the New York Academy of Medicine, provided the psychiatric nomenclature sub-section of the United States medical guide, the Standard Classified Nomenclature of Disease.

## DSM-I in 1952 —

During the Second World War, there was a most significant increase in psychiatric damage to American soldiers requiring their greater use of psychiatry in the selection, processing, assessment and treatment of soldiers. For this War did more than destroy a lot of real estate property, military resources, economies and dictatorial careers. There were perhaps as many as 62 million (a figure subject to controversy) men, women and children killed in combat, part of the collateral damage from combat or out of an ideological hatred of certain groups of people. It also created an immeasurable amount of damage to everyone else on all sides, damage that continues to this day all over the world. It may take a century or more just to recover from this War.

Moving away from mental institutions and traditional clinical perceptions, a committee headed by a psychiatrist, Brigadier General William C. Menninger (b. October 15, 1899; d. September 6, 1966), developed a new classification. Issued in 1943 as a War Department Technical Bulletin, under the support of the Office of the Surgeon General, it was the Medical 203.

The US Navy made some small revisions in DSM-I. Dealing with much more of the collateral damage and psychiatric issues from combat than the U.S. Navy, it was the U.S. Army who recognized a much greater need for a revision, to discard the Standard and to look at these psychiatric issues with more modern concepts and insights.

All of the U.S. Armed Forces accepted this new nomenclature eventually and, so did the Veterans Administration, with a tailored version of Medical 203.

It was in 1949, when the World Health Organization (WHO) published the sixth revision of the International

Statistical Classification of Diseases (ISCD), but for the first time, with a section on mental disorders.

A preface to DSM-1 identified their categorized mental disorders as similar to those of the U.S. Armed Forces' nomenclature. Then, given the power to develop a version for use in the United States, the Committee on Nomenclature and Statistics (CNS) standardized the dissimilar and bewildering treatment of different categories and classifications.

Then, in 1950, the same APA committee embarked on a review and discussion of its version. They then sent this version of Medical 203, the VA system and the Standard's Nomenclature, to approximately ten percent of every member of the APA.

Forty six percent replied. Ninety three percent of them approved of this version, and after some more revisions, it evolved into the DSM-I (Diagnostic and Statistical Manual -I). They approved of it in 1951 and then published it in 1952.

Configuration and conceptualizations were no different than they were in Medical 203, as many of the passages were nearly identical. This revised manual was 130 pages long and listed 106 mental disorders.

## In 1952—

Originally, in the 1952 edition of DSM-I, homosexuality listed as a *sociopathic personality disturbance*. Later, in 1962, it was a study entitled, "Homosexuality: A Psychoanalytic Study of Male Homosexuals", leading to the conclusion of homosexuality as a *"pathological hidden fear of the opposite sex caused by traumatic parent-child relationships."* [See Chapter Eight, An Exception to Defective Code in the Fantasy-Making Machinery, page 108] On face value, the medical profession accepted this study. Evelyn Hooker, however, a psychologist in 1956 and "The Mother of the Homosexual Movement," carried out a study comparing the *"happiness and well-adjusted nature of self-identified homosexual men with heterosexual men"* and, to everyone's surprise, found no difference.

This study flabbergasted the psychiatric community making her into a hero of the Gay and Lesbian community.

Nevertheless, homosexuality stayed in the DSM, listed as a psychiatric disorder, until May 1974.

## DSM-II in 1968 —

The 1960's saw many challenges to the concept and definition of mental illness. They came from psychiatrists, such as Thomas Szasz (b. April 15, 1920; d. September 8, 2012),[49] who reasoned mental illness as a myth we use to disguise our moral conflicts.

Sociologists, such as Erving Goffman (b. June 11, 1922; d. November 19, 1982)[50] said mental illness was merely an example of society labeling and controlling non-conforming people.

There were behavioral psychologists challenging the fundamental reliance of psychiatry on phenomena they could not observe and gay rights activists criticizing the listing of homosexuality as a mental disorder by the American Psychiatry Association in DSM-I.

There was another study published in Science by David Rosenhan (b. 1929; d. February 6, 2012)[51] who received a great deal of publicity of his study with his readers viewing it as an attack on the usefulness of psychiatric diagnosis.

In his obituary, dated February 16, 2012, the Stanford Law School blog said in their tribute of Professor Rosenhan: *"As part of his research study for 'On Being Sane in Insane Places,' Professor Rosenhan and seven others had*

---

[49] He was a well-known social critic of the moral and scientific foundations of psychiatry and of the social control of medicine in modern society, as well as of scientism. His books *The Myth of Mental Illness* (1960) and *The Manufacture of Madness* (1970) clarify some of his arguments on the subject.

[50] He was a Canadian-born sociologist and writer, thought of as "the most influential American sociologist of the twentieth century."

[51] He was an American psychologist best known for the Rosenhan experiment, a study challenging the validity of psychiatric diagnoses.

*themselves admitted as patients to a total of 12 mental hospitals during a three-year period. They described hallucinations and 'empty' feelings and were diagnosed as paranoid schizophrenics. As soon as they were admitted, they began acting normally and waited for the hospital staff to notice. The hospital staff never did notice, although many of the real patients caught on to the fakes. "*

The predominant psychodynamics (dynamic interplay) of psychiatry, plus certain biological viewpoints and theories, clearly revealed themselves in Kraepelin's (b. February 15, 1856; d. October 7, 1926)[52] system of classifications, in both DSM-I and DSM-II.

But, the symptoms for some specific disorders were vague in detail. They thought of some disorders as reflections of a more expansive underlying psychological conflict or a maladaptive reaction to life's problems. They thought of these problems as deep-seated in the distinction between neurosis and psychosis. They considered, roughly speaking, the anxiety/depression disorder (*neurosis*) as largely in touch with reality; and, on the other hand, the disorders of hallucinations/delusions (*psychosis*) come out as detached from reality, or a consistent distortion in the interpretation of reality.

Robert Spitzer (b. May 22, 1932)[53] and Joseph L. Fleiss (b. November 13, 1937; d. June 12, 2003)[54] wrote a paper, in 1974, *"clearly demonstrating the second edition of the DSM-II as an unreliable diagnostic tool."* Both of them found different practitioners using the DSM-II were hardly

---

[52] He was a German psychiatrist. H.J. Eysenck's Encyclopedia of Psychology identifies him as the founder of modern scientific psychiatry, as well as of psychopharmacology and psychiatric genetics.

[53] He is a retired professor of psychiatry and psychologist, and spent most of his career at Columbia University in New York City. He was on the research faculty for Psychoanalytic Training and Research, and was a major architect of the modern classification of mental disorders.

[54] He was a professor of biostatistics at the Columbia University Mailman School of Public Health, and also served as head of the Division of Biostatistics from 1975 to 1992. He was known for his work in mental health statistics, particularly assessing the reliability of diagnostic classifications, and the measures, models, and control of errors in categorization.

ever in accord with each other when diagnosing patients with similar problems.

In reviewing previous studies of 18 major diagnostic categories, Spitzer and Fleiss concluded: *"There are no diagnostic categories for which reliability is uniformly high. Reliability appears to be only satisfactory for three categories:* **mental deficiency**, **organic brain syndrome** (but not its subtypes), and **alcoholism**. The level of reliability is no better than fair for **psychosis and schizophrenia** and is poor for the remaining categories".*

## DSM - II in 1974 (Seventh printing) —

As covered earlier in this book, Ronald Bayer[55] was a psychiatrist and gay rights activist who protested against the APA in its 1970 convention in San Francisco.

He and other activists disrupted the conference, interrupted and even ridiculed any psychiatrists who articulated homosexuality as a mental disorder. Frank Kameny, a gay rights activist, working with the Gay Liberation Front in 1971, also demonstrated against the convention. He walked in front and grabbed the microphone from the speaker and shouted, *"Psychiatry is the enemy incarnate* [reducing the spiritual nature of homosexuality]. *Psychiatry has waged a relentless war of extermination against us. You may take this as a declaration of war against you* [against the homosexual community]."

This event occurred within the background of a much broader anti-psychiatry movement coming out to the forefront in the 1960's, out of recognition of a systematic abuse and pretentious, if not pompous, use of psychiatry, contesting the legitimacy of the APA's psychiatric methodologies,

---

* The use of **Bold** type is the author's decision to highlight and enhance communications.
[55] Very little biographical information is available on Ronald Bayer. Dr. Ronald Bayer, a pro-homosexual psychiatrist, has described what actually occurred in his book, *Homosexuality and American Psychiatry: the Politics of Diagnosis* (1981).

categories, classifications and diagnoses. Anti-psychiatry activists also protested at the same APA's convention with similar intellectual arguments as that of the homosexual activists.

Data from researchers, such as Alfred Kinsey and Evelyn Hooker, in the seventh edition of the DSM-II, subsequently no longer listed homosexuality as a mental disorder. With the trustees of the APA voting in 1973, and confirmed by the wider APA membership in 1974, *"sexual orientation disturbance"* replaced the earlier diagnosis.

## DSM-III in 1980 —

It was in 1974 when the APA made the decision to revise the DSM-II and to elect Robert Spitzer[53] as the chairman for this task force.

Initially, the driving force or purpose of this task force was to make the nomenclature in the new version of the DSM-III in concert with the International Statistical Classification of Diseases (SCD) and Related Health Problems, published by the World Health Organization.

Their principal goal was the uniformity and validity of psychiatric diagnoses throughout most of the world. In full view of the huge numbers of critics and criticisms, when no one could ignore the famous Rosenhan experiment, that was their primary objective. They needed to standardize the diagnostic practices within the US and Europe, and elsewhere, when research showed psychiatric diagnoses failed to agree conspicuously between Europe and the USA — or among themselves.

These measures were also an attempt to smooth the progress of the pharmaceutical regulatory process, a mess at the time.

The standards adopted for many of the mental disorders were taken from the Research Diagnostic Criteria (RDC)[56]

---

[56] A collection of psychiatric diagnostic criteria published in late 1970s with the purpose of allowing the diagnoses to be consistent in psychiatric research.

and Feighner Criteria,[57] recently developed by a group of research-orientated psychiatrists centered for the most part at Washington University in St. Louis and the New York State Psychiatric Institute.

Additional standards with, possibly, new categories of disorders, were recognized by consensus during the committee meetings, chaired by Robert Spitzer.[53] One of the main objectives was to build a catalog and system of classification of mental disorders using the conversational English language — easier for everyone to read — for effective communications.

A commonality among many, if not most, psychiatrists, including mathematicians and other scientific writers, is that they never took the time to learn to communicate in the written word. It is a combination of pretentiousness, with a pretentious vocabulary; exceedingly long sentences; the failure to use paragraphs appropriately and the common tendency to write to impress or to intimidate the reader instead of communicating with him.

Within a year, they completed the first draft of the DSM-III. Many new categories of disorders were included, but some deleted or changed. Then, almost immediately, a controversy surfaced concerning the deletion of the concept of neurosis. Neurosis is an important study of psychoanalytic theory and therapy; the DSM-III task force thought of it as ambiguous and unscientific in their standards.

In view of significant political opposition to the DSM-III, there was a serious threat of the APA Board of Trustees would not approve of it unless they did include Neurosis. In time, a political settlement resolved the problem.

Then, most interestingly, the task force replaced the diagnosis of "*sexual orientation disturbance*" with "*Ego-dystonic sexual orientation*,"an"*ego-dystonic mental disorder,*"defined as "*having a sexual orientation or an*

---

[57] **The Feighner Criteria** is the informal name given to diagnostic standards for use in psychiatric research published for the first time in a scientific paper in 1972. John Feighner was the principal author.

*attraction that is at odds with one's idealized self-image, causing anxiety and a desire to change one's orientation or become more comfortable with one's sexual orientation."*

Published in 1980, it was 494 pages long with a list of 265 diagnostic categories.

Immediately, it came into extensive use nationally and internationally; and was considered a revolution in the transformation of American psychiatry at the time.

## DSM-III-R in 1987—

DSM-III-R, in 1987, replaced DSM-III. Several categories got new names and reorganized with significant changes in their standards. With some others added, they deleted six categories. They also deleted certain controversial diagnoses, such as the *Pre-menstrual dysphoric disorder* and the *Masochistic personality disorder*.

DSM-III-R removed *"Sexual orientation disturbance"* and listed it under *"sexual disorder not otherwise specified,"* including *"persistent and marked distress about one's sexual orientation."*

Altogether, DSM-III-R contained 292 diagnoses and was 567 pages long.

## DSM-IV in 1994 —

DSM-IV, published in 1994, listed 297 disorders in 886 pages. It got much bigger with much more detail in their descriptions. A "steering committee," chaired by Allen Frances (b. 1942),[58] with 27 people, including four psychologists, formed 13 work groups of 5-16 members each with each work group consisting of approximately 20 advisers.

---

[58] He is an American psychiatrist better known for his chairing the task force that produced the DSM-IV.

Each group carried out an extensive literature review of their diagnoses.

Systematically, they requested data from researchers in order to conduct an analysis of the criteria they needed to change. With that data, they made serious changes from their earlier versions plus the requirement of a clinically significant standard to nearly half of the listed categories, a standard requiring *"clinically significant distress or impairment in social, occupational, or other important areas of functioning"* before listing it as a mental disorder.

They then removed some personality disorder diagnoses or moved them to the appendix of this edition. As we can see, the task force made significant changes in this edition in an honest attempt to be more objective, thorough, more readable and more useful to the psychiatric community.

## DSM-IV-TR in 2000 —

In the year of 2000, the APA revised DSM-IV. It was a "text revision" (hence "TR") of the DSM-IV called the DSM-IV-TR.

Very little of DSM-IV changed with the diagnostic categories with most of the specific criteria unchanged. The text sections gave successively more information on each diagnosis and then updated; then some of the diagnostic codes re-written to uphold uniformity with the International Classification of Diseases (ICD).

The APA organized DSM-IV-TR into a 5-part axial system: (1) the first axis included clinical disorders; (2) the second axis comprised of personality disorders and intellectual disabilities; and (3) the remaining three axes covered medical, psycho-social and environmental, and childhood issues necessary to provide diagnostic criteria for health care assessments.

## DSM-V or DSM-5 —

DSM-5 is the fifth edition of the Diagnostic and Statistical Manual of Mental Disorders published by the American Psychiatric Association.

DSM serves as a universal authority for the diagnosis of psychiatric disorders for the United States and many parts of the world. Treatment recommendations, as well as payment by health care providers, often determined by DSM classifications, meant the appearance of a new version would have significant practical importance.

The DSM-5 published on May 18, 2013, superseded the DSM-IV-TR. Development of the new edition began with a conference in 1999 and proceeded with the formation of a Task Force in 2007, which developed and field-tested a variety of new classifications. In most respects, DSM-5 changed not very much from DSM-IV-TR. Notable innovations include dropping Asperger Syndrome as a distinct classification; loss of subtype classifications for variant forms of schizophrenia; dropping the *"bereavement exclusion"* (such as the loss of a loved one due to death) for depressive disorders; a revised treatment and naming of *gender identity disorder* to *gender dysphoria* (hopelessness) and a new gambling disorder.

Various authorities criticized the 5th edition before and after its publication. The main thrust of criticism has been that changes in the DSM have not kept pace with advances in the study of psychiatric illnesses. The psychiatric drug industry has unfairly influenced the development of DSM-5 has been another criticism.

Many scientists argued the DSM-5 forces clinicians to make distinctions without real evidence, very serious distinctions with serious treatment repercussions, including drug prescriptions and health insurance coverage.

Such criticisms of the DSM-5 led to a petition signed by 13,000 people, sponsored by many mental health organizations, calling for an outside review of the document.

Another criticism is of psychiatry itself; the definition of mental disorder can include everything from a stress-induced anxiety to the schizophrenic personality of the paranoid type who hears voices. One condition is temporary and minor, and the other most definitely very serious and potentially dangerous to everyone, including himself.

With exceptions, such as birth defect, disease, mistreatment of medication or damage caused by the environment or trauma, most of these psychiatric illnesses will evaporate once the person recognizes and admits he has a problem, such as the inferiority complex. The biggest problem to these psychiatric illnesses is the stigma associated with them, making it very difficult for anyone to admit to any such problem. Many societies tend to treat such conditions as a moral or ethical defect in the personality, and any admission or recognition of a mental problem is enough to assume the worse in a person, even to deny him the right to possess firearms. Then there is that common problem of too many people judging themselves with one set of standards and with another, much higher set of standards, for judging everyone else -- particularly when dealing with psychiatric issues.

To put it in another way, a soldier in combat, facing the enemy, undergoing stress induced by the fear of the enemy shooting at him, or blowing him up with a mine or artillery round, could easily develop an anxiety disorder from it.

With those loose definitions of mental disorder, we could just as easily diagnose the soldier as mentally ill as a direct result of his going into combat when we ought to consider it as perfectly normal behavior for the condition he faced.

A young man or woman, in the last year of a 4-year college program, leading to an advance degree, would fit into the same category of mental disorder of a stress-induced anxiety directly resulting from his having to pass the final exam.

A man, husband and father, at the threshold of bankruptcy and losing his house, after losing his job, could also easily receive a diagnosis of a stress-induced anxiety. So, it is imperative to be very careful in our use of categories and classifications of mental disorders or, if not; we could easily destroy innocent and healthy people as well as our own credibility. Else; psychiatry becomes an assault weapon!

\*\*\*

# Chapter Seven

## *Controversies in the Categories, Classifications and Diagnosis of American Psychiatry*

As we can see in this brief history of the American Psychiatric Association's effort to categorize and classify mental disorders, it became immediately obvious their efforts turned into enormous problems full of controversy and complexity and, equally as obvious, much of it over their heads. Some of them pretended to know more than they did.

We have found people manipulating and intimidating the APA to declassify a mental disorder as perfectly normal behavior when unhappy with their classification; and other people critical of the psychodynamics of psychiatry: -- its way of doing things; or developing theories and systems of categories and classifications. Some people are even anti-psychiatry, understandably so with their experiences of people using psychiatry as an assault weapon against them to conceal crime or to suppress criticism of the state, or for some other sinister or suspicious reason. The improper and criminal use of psychiatry destroyed tens of thousands of people through a fraudulent diagnosis and false imprisonment in the 20th century, alone.

We have found everyone has a different opinion about everything and some people so strong with their views; they are willing to intimidate and bully everyone else for a common agreement with them.

Sometimes, the APA describes a mental condition as a mental disorder and, then, a few years later, in a subsequent edition of the DSM, after a considerable amount of discussion and argument beforehand, rescinds that same condition as no longer a mental disorder.

Some of these changes came with controversy and some only after a little discussion. Some of them caused nothing but discussion and controversy that continues even today, such as the proper category and classification of homosexuality. Even today, there is no consensus on this subject as to whether or not homosexuality is a perfectly normal behavior, within normal limits, or a serious psychiatric disorder. We have seen evidence the homosexual community intimidated the Association to remove homosexuality as a mental disorder in its Diagnostic and Statistical Manual.

We will find perfectly qualified psychiatrists, with all of their legal and medical credentials as psychiatrists with their diplomas, college degrees and certificates of accomplishments, who argue homosexuality as a mental disorder.

Then, we will find another group of perfectly qualified psychiatrists, with all of their legal and medical credentials as psychiatrists with their diplomas, college degrees and certificates of accomplishments, who argue homosexuality as normal human behavior (within normal limits, of course).

We will also find a pattern of the psychiatrists who argue homosexuality as a mental disorder to be heterosexual and the psychiatrists who argue otherwise to be homosexual.

There is no end to this controversy or the inconsistency in the definition of mental disorders!

In many parts of the world, particularly in the Muslims countries, with some important exceptions, homosexuality is a crime and subject to the death penalty if caught. In many other countries, there is a growing compassion for the homosexual community with recognition they are victims of a terrible medical condition not of their own fault.

In the 1952 edition of DSM, it listed homosexuality as a *"Sociopathic personality disturbance,"* and a study in 1962 led to the conclusion of homosexuality as a *"pathological hidden fear of the opposite sex caused by traumatic parent child relationships."*

In 1956, however, although the medical profession accepted this study, Evelyn Hooker, recognized today as "The Mother of the Homosexual Movement," proved it wrong with her study comparing the *"happiness and well-adjusted nature of self-identified homosexual men with heterosexual men,"* and, to everyone's surprise, found no difference. As reported, this study flabbergasted the psychiatric community and that made her into a champion for the Gay and Lesbian communities.

For years, the APA listed homosexuality as a Personality Disorder under DSM-II 302.0 — until 1973. Not until May of 1974 did the APA change its category and classification of homosexuality when some people, particularly the Gay rights activist, Frank Kameny, in 1971, demonstrated against the American Psychiatric Association in that years' convention.

In the 1960's, there were many challenges to the concepts and definitions of mental disorders. These challenges came from a variety of directions and authorities. One man, Thomas Szasz, a psychiatrist, argued mental disorders were *myths to disguise our moral conflicts.*

A sociologist, Erving Goffman, argued mental illnesses were simply a way by our societies to *label and control nonconforming people.*

There were people, such as David Rosenhan, who attacked the usefulness of psychiatric diagnosis. He conducted and participated in an experiment with seven other people in 12 different psychiatric hospitals during a three-year period. He quickly discovered the psychiatric staff never perceived him and his seven assistances, coming into the hospitals with phony diagnoses of the schizophrenic personality of the paranoid type, were faking it. Only the real patients caught onto the deception. The psychiatric staff, consisting of at least one psychiatrist and a crew of trained psychiatric technicians and nurses, could not tell the difference between the deception and the real schizophrenic personalities. Obviously, something is wrong with this science of psychiatry and its methods of analysis.

It is too subjective and uses a pretentious vocabulary leading to an interpretation more dependent on the personality type reading it than any systematic knowledge in the form of categories, classifications, explanations, testable theories and predictions about human normal or pathological behavior. At the same time, the American Psychiatric Association has made honest attempts to write in a more readable syntax and vocabulary without the pretentiousness in its Diagnostic and Statistical Manuals. There has been progress.

Nevertheless, that is not necessarily true with the bulk of our psychiatric literature. Much of it is unreadable and pretentious.

In Wikipedia, the free encyclopedia, it describes psychiatry in the following way.

*"Psychiatry refers to a field of medicine focused specifically on the mind, aiming to study, prevent, and treat mental disorders in humans. It has been described as an intermediary between the world from a social context and the world from the perspective of those who are mentally ill.*

*"Those who specialize in psychiatry are different than most other mental health professionals and physicians in that they must be familiar with both the social and biological sciences. The discipline is interested in the operations of different organs and body systems as classified by the patient's subjective experiences and the objective physiology of the patient. Psychiatry exists to treat mental disorders which are conventionally divided into three very general categories: mental illness, severe learning disability, and personality disorder. While the focus of psychiatry has changed little throughout time, the diagnostic and treatment processes have evolved dramatically and continue to do so. Since the late 20th century, the field of psychiatry has continued to become more biological and less conceptually isolated from the field of medicine."*

Then, it added a comment dealing with the abuse of psychiatry.

*"Controversy has often surrounded psychiatry, and the term anti-psychiatry was coined by psychiatrist* David Cooper *in 1967. The anti-psychiatry message is that psychiatric treatments are ultimately more damaging than helpful to patients, and psychiatry's history involves what may now be seen as dangerous treatments (e.g., Electroconvulsive therapy,[59] lobotomy[60]). Two charismatic psychiatrists who came to personify the movement against psychiatry were* R.D. Laing *and* Thomas Szasz. *Some ex-patient groups have become very anti-psychiatric, often referring to themselves as* 'survivors'".

In the 7th edition of DSM-II of 1974, as a direct result of the Gay rights activist, Frank Kameny, working with the Gay Liberation Front, part of a broader anti-psychiatry movement starting in the 1960s, which challenged the legitimacy of psychiatric diagnosis and its methodologies, no longer listed homosexuality as a mental disorder. These activists actually intimidated the APA. They offered no counter interpretation, theory or psychiatric analysis of homosexuality. They simply opposed the diagnosis of homosexuality as a mental disorder without an argument supporting their position. If not a mental disorder, then what is it? Being homosexual themselves, they simply objected to the categorization of *mental disorder* with its cultural connotations as "sick."

It was now a *"sexual orientation disturbance."* That would suggest a defective or damaged module in the DNA caused by sexual abuse as a child. See page 108, An Exception to Defective Code in the Fantasy-Making Machinery.

Just as interestingly, the DSM task force, working on DSM-III, replaced the diagnosis of homosexuality as a *"sexual orientation disturbance"* with *"Ego-dystonic* [ego

---

[59] **Electroconvulsive therapy** (ECT), formerly known as electroshock is a psychiatric treatment in which seizures are electrically induced in anesthetized patients for therapeutic effect.
[60] **Lobotomy** is a neurosurgical procedure, a form of psychosurgery, also known as a leukotomy or leucotomy. It consists of cutting or scraping away most of the connections to and from the prefrontal cortex, the anterior part of the frontal lobes of the brain. — Wikipedia, the free encyclopedia.

dis-tonic] *sexual orientation"* *(meaning in    conflict with the needs or goals of the ego)* and then described that as an *"ego-dystonic mental disorder."* It defined it as *"having a sexual orientation or an attraction that is at odds with one's idealized self-image, causing anxiety and a desire to change one's orientation or become more comfortable with one's sexual orientation."*

Properly speaking, that kind of definition is pure gobbledygook! It is also a complete contradiction to the earlier diagnoses of homosexuality since 1952. Nor does it necessarily explain anything, such as the cause and effect relationships.

Namely, what is homosexuality and what causes it?

There is clear evidence of an attempt by the APA to use pretentious jargon and mumbo jumbo to conceal their intellectual intimidation and dishonesty in a desire to avoid more controversy, as well as an honest desire to protect the homosexual community from societal abuses when they place the label of "mental disorder" on anyone or a particular mode of behavior. Such labels provide justification for some people to persecute people, or to even to murder them.

It also became dangerous for this Organization to discuss the subject in any other way, perhaps analogous to the days when intellectuals and scientists needed to write in code or anagrams to avoid the Spanish Inquisition. Almost everything they did or said evoked, provoked or elicited controversy, even among the experts.

Of course, they were not analyzing homosexuality, *per se*, but describing some of the symptoms of some people undergoing treatment for the confusion of their sexual orientation, perhaps by people who had been sexually abused during their formative years of development, or perhaps the kind of sexual abuse that interferes with the development of the mechanism responsible for the fantasy-making machinery, the machinery that determines our sexual orientation.

That made it worse! They were not really taking the time to study the subject properly, but receiving information from a variety of sources, some of it now clearly incompetent from people unable to recognize the difference between a person who entertains sexual fantasies with members of the same sex and persons not sure of the fantasy they ought to entertain or confused by their very existence.

What this means is that some people, aware of their sexual orientation, or aware of a confusion of their sexual fantasies they unsuspectingly, without a knowingly meaningful purpose, *experience* (not entertain) and with or without its corresponding effect over parts of their bodies (without understanding any of it or deriving any real pleasure from it) being different from that of the heterosexual community, of whom they intuitively perceive as the majority of the people, though not understanding their difference between everyone else, or the reasons for it, or the correct sexual fantasy for their gender and the sex of their body, nevertheless feel very uncomfortable with themselves – a very normal reaction.

It is that reaction the Task Force for DSM-III describes as a mental disorder. It is not the condition or cause of the condition, or an explanation for people who use the wrong sexual fantasy, or an explanation of the people confused with the sexual fantasies they do use or experience, but the reaction of the condition articulated by some members of a particular community.

In DSM-IV of    1994, a requirement established by the "steering committee" said, before we can declare a person as mentally ill, or identify a diagnosis as a mental disorder, there must be evidence of a "*significant distress or impairment in social, occupational, or other important areas of functioning*"

That means, before we can establish an anxiety, or a stress-induced anxiety, paranoia, delusions or any other diagnosis as a mental disorder, we must first establish significant distress or impairment of a person's relationship with other people and his environment.

An anxiety, or any other diagnosis, cannot be a mental disorder unless it first meets this standard. With that kind of standard, in the way written by this "steering committee," that would also include homosexuality as well as any other form of sexual orientation or gender identity confusion.

Obviously, there is a contradiction here with a major inconsistency. The contradiction is the actual definition of mental disorder. For a mental disorder to be a mental disorder, it is necessary to demonstrate that one's condition produces significant distress or an impairment of our relationship with others in our environment. Otherwise, the condition, such as a homosexual orientation or pedophilia, is not a mental disorder if it does not produce such an effect.

In other words, a person of a homosexual orientation (entertaining fantasies of sex with members of the same sex), or a pedophile (who entertains sexual fantasies with small children), is not mentally ill if he does not experience significant distress or impairment of his relationships with other people and his environment — as a result of his orientation. Many people would disagree with such a benchmark for determining mental illness.

Besides, although on the most part homosexuality is harmless with most people most of the time, pedophilia is not. Pedophilia is dangerous and can easily destroy a child, or children, entire families and the generations to come. It is not something we should take lightly.

The inconsistency is in the use of logic and the analysis of the reaction to a condition. Instead of an analysis of the cause of the condition, such as homosexuality or pedophilia, it examines only the effect of such a condition when such a person is either under treatment or facing criminal charges. That is not an intellectually and scientifically valid way of looking at things, though, perhaps understandable.

We must look at the cause of the condition as well as its effect. If a condition raises serious concerns with a person, causes serious problems for him with people and his environment, or represents an impediment to his personal relationships with people, then we must study and understand the cause of the condition in order to treat it. Or, else, we will have set off more problems than we can resolve — one of the major and basic criticisms of American psychiatry today.

Treatment is the ultimate goal and responsibility of psychiatry. Throughout the history of psychiatry, there has been that basic problem of psychiatry causing more damage than good to people with an urgent need for analysis and treatment and, sometimes, causing damage to healthy people with irresponsible psychiatric diagnoses and the reckless use of dangerous medications and treatments, including electroconvulsive therapy and Lobotomy, etc.

All too often, psychiatry has provided treatment based on ideology or street nonsense, instead of a legitimate analysis and science with the proper use of therapy, or recklessly using psychotropic medications that can easily turn toxic without conscientious care.

Now, it is clear there is only one cause of homosexuality. Mother Nature wrote out the DNA supporting the computer program module incorrectly for the sexual fantasy he would need for the correct sexual attraction for his gender and the sex of his body.

It is equally clear Mother Nature screws up on perhaps as many as 10 percent of the human population, possibly more. We may never know for sure.

We have, however, perhaps as many as several million people throughout the world using a dysfunctional sexual fantasy, such the sexual fantasies supporting Fetishism, Transvestitism, Exhibitionism, Voyeurism, Sadism, Masochism or Pedophilia and, until someone commits a crime and gets caught or requests medical or therapeutic treatment, we have no way of identifying him.

Nor does psychiatry have a way of unintrusively identifying such people, either.

\*\*\*

# Chapter Eight

## *The Sexual Fantasies We Use Determine our Sexual Orientation*

*Sexual orientation* is the final product of the sexual fantasy we use to motivate, navigate and drive our sexual attraction to persons of the opposite sex, to the same sex, to both sexes, or to animals (or to any combination of such).

A human being is a self-contained unit made up of millions of components, any of which can fail before our birth, at birth or substantially after birth. When we consider the enormous complexity of both our brain and body, with the millions of components, it is nothing short of miraculous that most of us are born healthy with everything working correctly.

We are also a binary system consisting of two genders. One gender is male and the other a female. Though each of us is self-contained, as reported in the above paragraph, Mother Nature designed us to work together as a single unit for procreation. It takes both units, working as one, for us to reproduce.

However, there is a technical problem here Mother Nature needed to work out beforehand a long time ago. How would we know enough to get together for the purpose of procreation? It is not natural, intuitive or instinctive. We do not come with an instruction manual, either. Nor is there any special or particular physical mechanism to attract us to each other and, in some respects, we might even perceive the opposite sex as repulsive, particularly if unwashed or ill mannered. As with some animals, we do not use a chemical odor emanating from a part of our body to bring us to the attention of the opposite sex. We do not use any mating sounds, colors, musical notes, calls or dancers. Our species is unique. We use fantasy.

*The Flirtation* (1904) is done by Eugene de Blaas, also known as **Eugene von Blaas** or **Eugenio Blaas** (July 24, 1843 — February 10, 1932). He was an Italian painter in the school known as Academic Classicism (a technique of painting and sculpture under the influence of the European academies of art). In this illustration, he clearly displays a heterosexual affection and attraction between members of the opposite sex -- in both directions. [Source: Wikipedia, the free encyclopedia]

Once we become of age, usually somewhere between 12 and 15 years, sometimes as young as eight years of age, there is a clock inside of us to turn on a computer program starting the process of our developing an attraction to the opposite sex.

This computer program is what manufactures the fantasy of sexual interplay with the opposite sex. A boy will start fantasizing sexual contact and interplay with a girl he may find particularly physically attractive and a girl, finding a boy attractive to her, will entertain a fantasy of making love to him.

If he knows enough about the subject, perhaps a more advance knowledge obtained from older boys, or knowledge from looking at pictures of naked women boys share with each other in the school's restrooms, or behind buildings, he may start off masturbating with a fantasy of touching her breast or in other erotic areas of her body. At first, it may not be a fantasy but a simple irritation or irritability of his penis. Once no longer physically and mentally active and in bed, trying to fall asleep, he finds his penis itching and growing in size, forcing him to reach down with his hand under the sheets to provide some measure of tranquility. Every night he would feel this same irritation and every night he would have to pacify it until, finally, he will have fallen asleep.

After a few days, however, there is a sudden release of tension. His pants, penis and hand are wet with no explanation. He is confused. He has had his first orgasm. It is extremely pleasant and almost immediately puts him asleep. From now on, to get asleep, he finds it necessary to masturbate almost every night — always an extremely pleasant experience.

For a girl, around the circumference of her clitoris, and her nipples, she may also feel an irritation or itching sensation causing her to soothe them with her fingers.

After a few nights of this, she may also accidentally discover an orgasm that immediately resolves her itching problem and puts her to sleep. After a few sessions, it will not take her long to realize she can get to sleep much more easily and faster with her masturbating fingers. Within a few minutes, it always leads to a pleasant and fulfilling orgasm.

Every child, boy or girl, is a little different and, therefore, may have a slightly different experience. Still, there is that same pattern as each of us grows up into an adult.

All of this is normal behavior and very important for every boy and girl.

About that time, before, during or after, both of them will begin to entertain a fantasy of making love to an attractive member of the opposite sex with greater consistency and regularity, although some of them may perceive it as "sinful" or indicative of an illness (depending on their culture and religion, and the child). Most of them will be mature enough, however, to recognize masturbation and fantasy as normal. Some will not, of course, and this may create some anxiety for them, as there would be no one, other than perhaps a mother or (very) close friend, to help them to understand it as perfectly normal behavior for their age. Usually, they work it out on their own over a period of time.

It entails their using a fantasy to aide in their masturbation long enough to elicit an orgasm and then to fall asleep. This heterosexual pattern of sexual maturity, from a child growing into an adult, is almost exactly the same with each of us. It will vary only a little in detail.

As each child continues to develop and mature into a young adult, his fantasies will vary, evolve and get richer in detail and, each time, will continue to motivate, navigate and drive him into, eventually, a sexual and long-term relationship with the opposite sex.

Culture plays an important part in this pattern of maturation. As he continues to mature, his culture provides a "path" for him. His culture directs him onto the path of finding a woman to marry and to start a family with her with their children.

She receives a corresponding cultural program to find an acceptable man to marry, to start a family and to give birth to his children.

There is a genetic computer program inside each of us to fantasize sex with a member of the opposite sex and a culturally induced fantasy fantasying a family with children of our own. This origin of a cultural variable influencing or modulating our sexual fantasies, and creating a fantasy of its own for us to start our own family, probably goes back more than 200,000 years ago — and probably well before the introduction our own species.

## Some Important Exceptions—

Sometimes Mother Nature really screws up. Sometimes, when a child becomes of age, his internal clock fails to work correctly. It fails to turn on his fantasy-making computer. Though there may or may not be the sensation of irritation or irritability in the penis or clitoris, there is no fantasy accompanying it, the fantasy or the engine to motivate, navigate and drive us toward a sexual attraction with the opposite sex. Sometimes there is no such sensation of irritation or irritability, either.

It leaves the person in a state of perpetual confusion as he grows up into adulthood. After a period

Shulamith Firestone (b. January 7, 1945; d. August 28, 2012) [Fair Use]

of time, the child, almost an adult by then, may perceive something a little different about himself in comparison to everyone else his age. Still, he does not understand it. With no one around to help him to understand it, either, or a 800 toll-free telephone call to make for technical support, he is left to his own devices without a clue, other than what he can perceive externally looking at and listening to people.

Perhaps one example of a person without a working fantasy-making computer would be Shulamith Firestone (b. January 7, 1945; d. August 28, 2012). She was a Canadian-born feminist and a central figure in the early development of radical feminism.

She, in 1970, wrote *"The Dielectric of Sex: The Case for Feminist Revolution."* At that time, some feminists considered it an important and influential text on feminism. Today, some of them now recognize it as an ignorant and preposterous hypothesis of human sexuality.

She wanted to eliminate "sex roles, procreative sex, gender, childhood, monogamy, mothering, the family unit … and the physiological phenomena of pregnancy and childbirth."[61] See *"Eulogy for a Sex Radical: Shulamith Firestone's Forgotten Feminism."*

In Wikipedia, the free encyclopedia, she wrote:

> *"Firestone argued* gender inequality *originated in the* patriarchal *societal structures* imposed upon women through their biology; the physical, social and psychological disadvantages imposed by pregnancy, childbirth, and subsequent child-rearing. She advocated the use of cybernetics to carry out human reproduction in laboratories as well as the proliferation of contraception, abortion, and state support for child rearing; enabling them to escape their biologically determined positions in society. She described pregnancy as "barbaric", and writes that a friend of hers compared labor to 'shitting a pumpkin'. Among the reproductive technologies she predicted were sex selection and in vitro fertilization."

In The Dialectic of Sex, she wrote:

> *"So that just as to assure elimination of economic classes requires the revolt of the underclass (the proletariat) and, in a temporary dictatorship, their seizure of the means of production, so to assure the elimination of sexual classes requires the revolt of the underclass (women) and the seizure of control of reproduction: not only the full restoration to women of ownership of their own bodies, but also their (temporary) seizure of control of human fertility — the*

---

[61] Source: Wikipedia, the free encyclopedia http://www.theatlantic.com/national/archive/2012/08/eulogy-for-a-sex-radical-shulamith-firestones-forgotten-feminism/261834/

*new population biology as well as all the social institutions of child-bearing and child-rearing. And just as the end goal of socialist revolution was not only the elimination of the economic class privilege but of the economic class distinction itself, so the end goal of feminist revolution must be, unlike that of the first feminist movement, not just the elimination of male privilege but of the sex distinction itself: genital differences between human beings would no longer matter culturally. A reversion to an unobstructed pansexuality Freud's 'polymorphous perversity'—would probably supersede hetero/ homo/bi-sexuality.) The reproduction of the species by one sex for the benefit of both would be replaced by (at least the option of) artificial reproduction: children would [be] born to both sexes equally, or independently of either, however one chooses to look at it; the dependence of the child on the mother (and vice versa) would give way to a greatly shortened dependence on a small group of others in general, and any remaining inferiority to adults in physical strength would be compensated for culturally. The division of labour would be ended by the elimination of labour altogether (through cybernetics). The tyranny of the biological family would be broken."*
[Source: Wikipedia, the free encyclopedia]

If we were to examine her account of human sexuality, with her attempt to incorporate the theories of Sigmund Freud, Wilhelm Reich, Karl Marx, Frederick Engels and Simone de Beauvoir into a radical feminist theory of politics and socialist ideologies, it becomes immediately obvious she was very intelligent and had done a lot of reading. However, at the same time, there was an obvious relationship between her attempt to synthesize all of these theories and ideologies to her personality contradictions to the world around her.

She was different from most women around her and obviously knew it. She did not understand the reason, of course. Nor was there anyone to tell her. Even if someone were to recognize her psychiatric condition, there was nothing anyone could have done to help her. We do not have the science and support systems to help anyone with this kind of problem; either then or now.

The clue pops out conspicuously when we read a little more about her biography. She wanted to "eliminate gender" and, in the process of her argument, distorted some ideology from Marxism with the view *"that all forms of oppression were rooted in an antagonism between men and women."* Then she added, *"Resolving this antagonism would pave the road to utopia and cure society of its ills."* Most women would not have agreed with her. Additionally, seventy-four years of Communism in the Soviet Union and elsewhere will easily destroy any notion it works; her "synthesis" of Communism with her personality contradictions will not work, either. Blending nonsense with a dysfunctional sexual orientation program creates only a larger body of nonsense while failing to address the source of her dysfunction.

Communism is an ideology, or system of rationalizing nonsense, based on both a jealousy and hatred of an imperfect system of economics full of conspicuous wealth, poverty, economic power, wrongs and injustices without ethical regulations.

Her personality contradictions were the product of Mother Nature not turning on a sexual orientation program for her. It left her in a constant state of turmoil and, obviously, with no help from anyone, looking around in world literature for an explanation, she thought she found one with a theory of economics, not recognizing it as fraud and a system of intellectual rationalizations.

Unlike most women, she felt no attraction to men, a desire to make love to a man or to give birth to his child (of which she may have perceived as repulsive). Most little girls, as young as eight to 12 years of age, normally entertain romantic fantasies of giving birth to children, while imitating their mothers, even while still too young to masturbate or to entertain sexual fantasies. To her, it was a *"battle of the sexes"* and the source of all injustices and inequalities. She did not want to destroy all men, or to eliminate them entirely although, admittedly, she did not like them very much, either.

She perceived man's power to define and control the relationship with woman to be an error in nature and an unnatural abuse of power over woman, though it certainly can be but not necessarily so. She failed to either recognize or understand it is the woman who defines and controls the development of the family and child, though that certainly can also lead to unnatural abuse but not necessarily so.

It is unlikely she could even perceive or, if she could, to understand most women incorporate man's power to define and control the relationship with them in their sexual fantasies. His power to control her does not deter her, either, as long as he treats her with gentle persuasiveness in her fantasies — and in real life; and their sexual fantasies complement each other as a precondition for their relationships to work properly.

When we look at and compare the power relationship between man and woman, something she could never do, it becomes very obvious Mother Nature has created equality between man and woman in a working binary relationship: -- Man defines and controls the relationship with her and she defines and controls the family he provides for her. Hence, they are equal to each other in this binary relationship, though both of them can and frequently do abuse each other, or may not even understand their relationship as a working binary relationship. Many men have difficulties understanding their role in this kind of relationship and many women fail to understand the enormous difficulties for a man to fulfill his responsibilities in his role. Nor is it easy for her in her role, either, of course.

However, for this relationship of equality between man and woman to work, it is necessary for the man to entertain both a sexual fantasy with a woman and a cultural fantasy of a family with her with children, and for her to entertain a sexual fantasy with a man and a cultural fantasy with a family with him and children. Otherwise, such a binary relationship cannot work. To be successful, both of them must be willing and able to make a commitment to each other for life, or most of it, in a team relationship sharing each other's sexual fantasies. That is love.

She, on the other hand, may grow up with low self-esteem thinking only the man has power, and jealous of his power to define and control the relationship with her, without any recognition of her corresponding power to modulate the control he has over her.

Some women may incorporate the man's power to control her into an integral part of her sexual fantasy and other women may waste their entire lives fighting it.

Some boys and some girls never grow up to recognize the *natural balance* in the power relationship between man and woman and, of course, both of them may find the *"grass greener on the other side of the fence,"* even when nothing is genetically wrong with their brains and bodies.

Analogous to the person trying to perfect the *"perpetual motion machine"*, which ignores certain critical laws of physics to make it possible, they ignore the laws of managerial science, if aware of them, which our power must correspond with our roles and responsibilities. Though it can be abusive, if we use it incorrectly, it has the purpose to provide us with the power to carry out our roles and responsibilities.

Likewise, if we were to assign a person to a position in management, we would have to provide a *balance of power and authority with responsibility* in order to allow him to carry out his responsibilities properly. If he lacks the power and authority to carry out his responsibilities, or to make decisions, he gets nothing done. If he has too much power and authority for his level of responsibility, however, it consistently leads to abuse, and we have a long history of such abuses going well into prehistory to prove the validity of that statement.

Nor is there any exception in the power relationship between man and women, either. There must be a balance between  power and responsibility, the power and responsibility given to us by the role we must play  for  the sex Mother Nature has assigned to us.

From this material, it seems very apparent her internal clock did not turn on her fantasy-making computer program. She may or may not have masturbated and, if she did, may or may not have experienced orgasms. One thing is certain, however; she held no physical or sexual attraction to men for the lack of a sexual fantasy to motivate, navigate and drive her into a sexual relationship. This attraction, she could evidently perceive from watching other men and women in the public, was probably incomprehensible to her, if not genuinely repulsive.

## Normal Heterosexual Fantasy —

In normal or with most heterosexual persons, who routinely experience and use sexual fantasy, it is predominately a fantasy of sex and sexual interplay with a member or members of the opposite sex with only a slight variation from day-to-day.

It usually entails sexual fantasy accompanying foreplay or masturbation ending in an orgasm. An orgasm is the objective.  Fantasy drives the foreplay or masturbation into the direction of an attraction toward the opposite sex for the purpose of sexual gratification, intercourse and children.

However, there are many instances of boys and girls, while growing up into men and women, who briefly entertained the wrong sexual fantasy for their gender and sex without their causing harm to themselves. Some may grow up briefly without using a fantasy of any kind and others may develop a broad capability of fantasizing sex with men, women or animals without harm, while consciously switching back and forth to accommodate their need or desire for an orgasm during masturbation or even intercourse — in order to reach an orgasm.

## Defective Code in the Fantasy-Making Machinery —

Apparently, there are also some people, on the basis of

what I can perceive while studying this subject, with the DNA code in their fantasy-making computer program so severely damaged, instead of fantasizing sex with a man, woman or animal, it is a fantasy, or a partial fantasy, that does not develop into a recognizable image of any kind. Yet, partial or not, and without a recognizable image to provide the proper drive and direction, it nevertheless generates enough sexual tension they can only release through physical masturbation without the aide of a properly working fantasy. This causes intense frustration and confusion; and they have no clue or anyone to help them.

## An Exception to Defective Code in the Fantasy-Making Machinery –

In the last few year I have personally observed, or think I did, the distinctive possibility of sexual abuse of a child, during his formative years, for it to have interfered and damaged the genetic code responsible for the development of his *sexual orientation identity* – separate from the genetic defects described above. A recent observation and study of a young man, who had been sexually abused by his step-father during his critically formative years, found him projecting his hate, anger and rage over this experience many years earlier onto two perfectly innocent people, a selection process he apparently made almost randomly. Just as interestingly, he was under psychiatric care from a team of specialists who encouraged him, as part of his treatment, to file charges against these two people of whom he accused of sexually abusing him, but without their realizing it as a projection of his hate, anger and rage. They can be that naïve -- and dangerous, too!

## Born with the Wrong Brain —

Some, unfortunately, were born with the sex of their brain the opposite of the sex of their body. At an early age, they may perceive something wrong with themselves. Their brain is of one sex and their body of the opposite sex. To be successful, of course, the sex of their body must match the sex of their brain and, when it does not, there is nothing but constant turmoil for that person for the rest of his life.

When I was in the 5th grade during a period of recess in the back of the school building, I recall one boy, who was not a friend, or even an acquaintance; approach me with the following statement, while pointing down to his penis, *"What is that thing doing there?"*

It took me a long while for me to understand he had a boy's body but a girl's brain. His turmoil, though too young for me to realize it at the time, must have been enormous. I never saw him again. Often, I think about him (or her) and wonder if he had somehow adjusted to his condition. After years of studying this subject, I think it is most unlikely.

No one can help him and medical science has nowhere near the expertise necessary to make any corrections for him, such as the expertise to re-write the DNA code to match the sex of his body to the sex of his brain. He may have spent the remaining of his life fighting the problem and the culture where he lives. If a hostile culture, as is common in many parts of the world, he spent his life in misery under enormous stress with little or no sympathy or understanding from anyone, least of all his parents, siblings and relatives.

## Switching Gender Back and Forth —

Then there is the person, whose brain switches gender from male to female back and forth, as if to say, "I'm a man. No, I'm a woman. No, I'm a man,"... and so on. The sex of his body stays constant while the sex of his brain switches back and forth randomly, unable to select a gender (sex) consistent and compatible with the sex of his body. As we can well imagine, his confusion, frustration and stress would be enormous. Under such circumstances, a stable and comfortable life is impossible for him with no sympathy or insight from anyone, either. Nor is medical science advance enough to treat the problem — or even to recognize it.

## Switching Gender out of Amusement —

Some people may enjoy switching their gender as, if to say, a joy for them, a recreation, amusement, hobby or play of switching gender from, say, a female for a few hours in the morning immediately after getting up out of bed and, then, in mid-day or the afternoon, a male for the rest of the day. They do not seem to suffer any great anxiety or stress in this ability to switch gender to suit their mood for the day — or for the moment. Nor do they seem to understand the reason for this "capability," either; -- nor to care. For them, that is their life and they seem comfortable with it.

## The Male Homosexual —

Then there is the male homosexual. He is a man and has a man's brain with a man's body. The only thing that makes him different from the heterosexual man is the sexual fantasy he uses. He predominately entertains a fantasy of sex with other men instead of women. That makes him into a homosexual male instead of a heterosexual male. It may be a sexual fantasy of oral sex with other men or, in some instances, oral sex with male animals, such as horses and zebras. They have long penises. It "turns him on," although it may have no such effect on a heterosexual male. In fact, it may repel a heterosexual male even if he has the ability or flexibility to fantasize oral sex with other men or animals; such a fantasy simply fails to arouse him. In some instances, as with normal heterosexual men, there is an ability to entertain sexual fantasies with women but without the fantasy arousing them.

## The Female Homosexual —

Then there is the female homosexual. She has a female body and a female brain but predominately uses a sexual fantasy of sex with other women instead of men. That makes her into a homosexual female instead of a heterosexual female. In this instance, women "turn her on" sexually. She entertains sexual fantasies of oral sex with other women, but a man's penis may or may not do a thing for her, though she may be jealous of it and its power to control women.

With some exceptions, male homosexuality causes little or no problems in society today, other than to irritate society with its incompatible sexual orientation and affection toward men, and they face far more severe discrimination and persecution than female homosexuals, or, for that matter, any other dysfunctional sexual orientation, including pedophilia.

Female homosexuality, on the other hand, has been responsible for a wide variety of societal problems. Perhaps the most conspicuous problem by the Lesbian community has been their demand for *"equality"* between the sexes while portraying themselves as normal heterosexual women seeking justice for all of the wrongs and injustices done to women by men. In this representation, they will ignore the wrongs and injustices done to men by women, if they can perceive it at all. Though they cannot perceive it, the power relationship between man and woman works in both directions. In a heterosexual relationship, they have power over each other and, with this power, frequently abuse it. At the same time, they work as a team living for each other as they travel together through life sharing each other's problems and resolving them together.

Even when they do not openly portray themselves as heterosexual, they consciously allow people to think of themselves as heterosexual, while carefully avoiding a discussion of their sexual orientation toward a preference for sex with other women, knowing it would immediately alienate people.

While they argue equal pay for equal work for women, a perfectly valid position, they demand government and private industry employ women in positions of high responsibility, top management and top pay with men. They ignore the original reason behind the differences in the pay scale between men and women were a demand by women in a subservient role to their husbands working to supplement his income. These women did not want their husbands to perceive them as competing with them. They just wanted enough additional income in the family to make an important difference. It had nothing to do with gender discrimination or fraud.

As Pope John Paul II discovered in his research, this kind of argument "blurs" the distinction between the two sexes and treats both sexes as if there were no physical or psychological differences between them. But there are enormous differences; and the roles we must play, in a heterosexual relationship, are very much different than from the roles between Lesbian couples — or between Gay men.

Nevertheless, their arguments and subsequent demands translate into political pressure to select women over men in many critical managerial positions in the government, even if not qualified.

There are instances of a state or federal agency looking for a manager to fill a vacancy. When the deadline arrives, with no woman applying for this position for an evaluation, after they will have selected the best-qualified man for the position, some women activists have argued the agency should have waited until a woman applies — and then hire her. It does not make any difference if the woman qualifies or not as long as the agency proves its commitment to *"equality"* between the sexes.

There are several serious ramifications behind such a demand for this kind of *"equality."* Most notably, since it is man's responsibility to work and to support the family in a heterosexual relationship, this kind of *"equality"* actually discriminates against heterosexual relationships and heterosexual men and women.

Another ramification is a more sinister repercussion of an agency, such as the Veterans Administration, under constant political pressure to hire women in their demonstration of a commitment to *"equality,"* will hire and place several women in the same chain-of-command over men in a given medical facility. Remember! The Veterans Administration is a federal agency with the purpose of providing medical service and treatment to men and women with non-service and service-connected medical disabilities. However, the patients are predominately men.

It becomes sinister when the hiring managers ignore the male applicants to hire only female applicants due to political pressure to hire women. Since most heterosexual women have commitments to their husbands and children, few of them would in be a position to accept long hours working in high-pressured managerial positions (except for much older women with their children grown up and out of the house). That means most of the women available to accept such positions would be lesbians without the responsibility of a husband and children.

A case in point would be an incident that occurred a few years ago in West Haven, Connecticut. In the basement of Building #1, there is the Woman's Health Center. At the time, you will have seen a small hand-written note on the door saying,

"NO MEN ALLOWED WITHOUT A WOMAN'S PERMISSION."

I hold a service-connected disability occurred during the Vietnam War and my wife, as a spouse, has almost the same benefits. At the time, she was seriously ill. I took her to this VA clinic for an examination and diagnosis of her medical condition.

Eventually, she had an operation outside of Boston.

When we had arrived through the front door of this clinic, a female secretary immediately confronted me, "Do you have a woman's permission to be here?" I replied, "I do not need anyone's permission to be with my wife." Then, both of us walked into her assigned doctor's office. As we sat down in her office, I overheard her female doctor whispering to my wife while looking at me with the corner of her right eye, "Is it alright for that man to be here with you?"

My wife responded in a surprised voice,    **"He's my husband!"** I said nothing but listened and watched her carefully.

We were in this clinic for approximately one hour. After

about 15 minutes with my wife, I stood up and walked out of the office in order to examine of what I could perceive as a serious pathological condition in this clinic.

In the Waiting Room, there were several women waiting for their turn to see a doctor. I could easily perceive them as average female heterosexuals. Two of them were seriously obese. None of them found it objectionable for me to be there in their presence. Although another woman was a little overweight, she was also very attractive — and knew it. She enjoyed being a woman and the power to influence men with her sex appeal. Another woman radiated subservience to man and also enjoy the power that comes with it.

Only the secretary objected. Before my wife and I left the reception area, I looked at her carefully. Without forming any immediate conclusion or opinion, with the intention of absorbing as much information as possible before leaving her office, I noticed her eyes were red and blood-shot. Her skin was a pale white and she also was a little overweight.

As my wife and I walked down the corridor to the stairwell and up to the cafeteria, my wife served me notice she would no longer go to that place. She said, "This place is *'weird'* and some of those women *'strange'*." She wanted nothing to do with them or with the hospital. It was my wife's first encounter with militant feminists and she did not like it.

Later, I located another facility for her with a woman's clinic just outside of Boston.

As we approached the cafeteria on the 1st floor, I began to form relationships in that recent event down in the basement from the information absorbed earlier. The secretary had an inferiority complex. I then became aware she was afraid of men — and me in general. She was not eating correctly, either, probably the wrong kind of foods and nutritionally out of balance for her body needs. Her eyes and body English communicated hate, anger and rage toward men out of jealousy of men.

We ate our lunch, and while waiting for her next appointment at 1:00 o'clock, I continually thought about that experience and continued to form relationships. While walking through that clinic and elsewhere throughout the Hospital, I discovered there was a disproportionate number of female employees who were lesbians, though most of them not man-haters. Some of them were still struggling with their true sexual identity and purpose in life. Some of them seemed to have accepted themselves as different from most women.

When we got home, over the next few days, I made a few telephone calls in West Haven to file a complaint of mistreatment against my wife and me. It was then I discovered the entire chain-of-command in the managerial department contained almost all women and made up predominately of lesbians. In fact, none of them, with the exception of a heterosexual female working as a secretary for the Director, would communicate with me in order to listen to my complaint. She was clearly aware of the high concentration of lesbians in that facility — and said so. The Patient Advocate, however, would not even respond to my telephone inquiries, the person in each VA facility who represents patients with a complaint against a VA employee (but lacks the real authority to do anything). It is a fraud!

Here is an instance of several women, with female brains and female bodies, using the wrong sexual fantasy. They fantasize sex with other women instead of men and, in the process, developed an anti-male ideology. They developed this ideology out of jealousy of man; then converted the jealousy into hate. Unable to separate themselves from man's power, they created a little microcosmic world of their own without a man to interfere with their relationships with each other as they enjoyed their fantasies of making love to each other.

Unable to use the correct sexual fantasy for their gender, they were unable to accept a sexual relationship with a man. Therefore, they were unable to understand the binary relationship between a man and a woman or to share his fantasies. Their fantasies drove them into relationships with each other and repelled any idea of a relationship with men.

The whole idea of a sexual relationship with men was disgusting and, yet, they were jealous of him, his superior strength and his power to control them. That jealousy led to hatred, anger and, finally, rage. As long as they kept to themselves in this microcosmic world, they were safe; however, once they will have left their world, or a man were to enter it, they felt a threat from him. For they will have lost their power to him.

Another ramification to this homosexuality is readily available to observe on television almost every day. Under constant pressure to demonstrate a commitment to *"equality"* between the sexes, our entertainment industry has become part of the problem. In an attempt to alter the relationship or to *"blur"* the distinction between man and woman in a heterosexual relationship, now, on a daily basis, they depict women beating the hell out of men and making them look stupid while women actors talk down to them, talk over them and, generally, dominate the conversations.

In one notable example, we can look at James Bond 007, an action fantasy for men originating from a real secret agent during the Second World War fighting the Nazis. In the last few episodes, without any transition or meaningful explanation, his boss is now a woman who talks down to him while describing him as a *"male chauvinist pig."* Even Miss Moneypenny, who in earlier episodes was depicted as a woman in love with James Bond and fantasizing making love to him, is now shooting daggers at him while also calling him a *"male chauvinist pig."*

Whether or not the homosexual community wants to accept homosexuality as a mental disorder, the fact remains it is not normal human behavior for most people and those depictions lead us to nowhere.

Now, since the late 1970's, when the American Psychiatric Association removed homosexuality as a mental disorder from its Diagnostic and Statistical Manual, the homosexual community has built a significant powerbase to significantly influence — not just public opinion — but politics, the entertainment industry and law.

They demand equal treatment under law and complete acceptance of their assertive right for same-sex marriages. Of course, we cannot effectively argue against equal treatment under law. They are human beings and have the same inherent rights as any other human being, whether mentally ill or not. Even the assertive right for same-sex marriages would be difficult for anyone to argue against it. They have a right for fair and honest treatment with a show of a little compassion, as Pope Francis argued recently.

Many years earlier, Pope John Paul II said, after defending the Catholic Church's opposition to same-sex marriages, that people with a homosexual orientation *"possess the same inherent dignity and rights as everybody else."* Even then, almost immediately after Pope Francis made this same declaration for compassion, years after Pope John Paul II, there were members of the homosexual community criticizing Pope Francis for not accepting homosexuality as normal behavior or allowing same-sex marriages in the Catholic Church.

However, the 14th Dalai Lama, Lhamo Dondrub, an exile from Tibet, recognized the human rights of homosexuals to exit in peace and to marry members of the same sex.

This problem is not, in this issue of controversy, a question of civil rights and equality, but a situation in which the entire subject has evolved into an ideology. If you do not agree with them, then you are a *"male chauvinist pig,"* whatever that is supposed to mean.

I have even seen instances of militant feminists calling women, in a debate on television, who argued in opposition to their positions, a *"male chauvinist pig."*

Over a period of more than 30 years, the world, with some important exceptions, particularly the Muslim world in the Middle East, has slowly grown into tolerance for homosexuality. Along with a compassion for the people with this problem, there is a growing recognition the homosexual community, as do every other human community, consist of human beings. They have the same rights as everyone else. Treating them differently violates the concept of human rights and American constitutional civil rights.

However, as the world grows more tolerant of homosexuality, the Lesbian community has grown less tolerant of anything less than complete acceptance of them as normal and, in some respects, complete acceptance of their superiority over the heterosexual community, such as superiority over heterosexual women raising their own children. They think they can do a better job at it. It is not just complete acceptance of their homosexuality, moreover, but a demand of a reversal of the power relationship between man and woman. They want to make the woman in this relationship dominant and the man subservient to her.

That becomes obvious when we watch prime-time movies and comedies on television every evening. Notice it is the woman who dominates every conversation and the entire relationship while the man plays the part of the fool in a subservient role. Interestingly, most heterosexual women, including teenage girls, do not accept this dominant position, as they can readily perceive the fraud, although they may not understand the reasons or ulterior motives behind it.

Nor do they always completely understand the roles they ought to play, confusion caused by our entertainment industry. They are just happy to receive an honest and fair treatment from men. Many women enjoy the subservient role and their power to modulate the control man has over them through their sexual attractiveness. Even unattractive women have this power over men — and they know it. Sometimes, that power to modulate man's power over them can lead to much abuse. Most women know that, too. Almost every woman has a memory of seeing another woman abusing a man with the power of her sexual attractiveness, or a man abusing a woman with his superior strength.

Notice, also, you will find a strange contradiction in the visual representation of women in these Hollywood productions. Though they are portrayed as dominant in the relationship with man, they wear clothing and makeup appropriate for a woman in a subservient role dressed to attract men with their sex appeal, a most significant contradiction.

Nearly 30 years ago, we have had a similar situation of the writers and producers of prime- time television incorporating anti-gun messages in their productions every evening. For several years, we could not watch television without seeing them constantly. A few years ago, the National Rifle Association reported certain anti-gun organizations were trying to enlist the services of these writers and producers to incorporate again similar anti-gun messages. They wanted to repeat their earlier successes of the late 1970's and early 1980's.

It does not take much imagination or thought to realize some of these writers and producers were accepting bribes to write anti-gun messages. It was certainly no accident or happenstance of our suddenly finding anti-gun messages everywhere on television every evening. That took collusion through the formal agreement. Nor does it take any imagination or true paranoia to realize, for the last few years, we have had precisely the same pattern of collusion between Hollywood and the militant feminists to socially engineer a change in the relationship between man and woman (while ignoring our genetic makeup and the purpose behind our binary system).

Notice, however, they did not develop their knowledgebase on a science but an ideology, and used that ideology as the core of their motivation and drive in these manipulations and cunning communications. All the while they ignored the available science.

We can argue some of these actors are fools themselves. They should think it out before they accept such roles and to consider the repercussions in society before signing a contract.

Notice, also, the enormous number of people unable to perceive these *"messages"* as collusion to socially engineer a change in society but, instead, interpret it as a legitimate recognition of society's efforts to correct all the wrongs and injustices done to women by men.

It is one thing for society to show compassion for homosexuality, whether a mental disorder or not, and another entirely different thing to allow the Lesbian community to alter the relationship between man and woman in order to accommodate an ideology motivated, shaped and driven by an inferiority complex.

## The Sexual Predator —

There are many different varieties of sexual predators throughout the world, some of them exceedingly dangerous, even evil, and others just plain offensive to our moral senses.

During the 1920's, it was the FBI Director, J. Edgar Hoover, who may have used the term, *"Sexual Predator,"* for the first time.

Since that time, there have been several legal definitions of this term, inside and outside of courts, by local and state governments.

In American law, throughout the United States, "sexual predator" and "sex offender" have distinct, sometimes contradictory, definitions. Many states use them differently from each other, some of it abusively and full of contradictions and inconsistencies.

Legally, in most instances, a sexual offender is a person who commits a sexual offense as defined under their law. A sexual predator, on the other hand, refers to a person who consistently seeks out sexual situations we deem as exploitative to the victim, something he takes away from his victim without giving anything back of equal value. It may be a man who entertains a sexual fantasy of sex with an attractive young woman and, without any thought or consideration to her needs and feelings, exploits her vulnerability to him for his own sexual gratification. She gets nothing out of it except pain and bad memories.

He could be a person who targets certain kinds of young women naïve in the ways of sex and sexual relationships. Once he has had his way with her, he abandons her for another victim. If he gets her pregnant, he denies all responsibility and walks away from her, sometimes leaving behind in his life several women burden with the responsibility of raising his children without his financial and emotional support and -- without any remorse.

A sexual predator could also be a young middle-age woman, afraid and unwilling to make love with a man of her own age, who has the power to define and control the relationship with her and, for this reason, seeks out young boys too young to control the relationship but old enough to perform sexually for her. Then, as he matures and discovers his power to define and control this relationship, she abandons him for a younger boy. Each time, she fulfills her sexual fantasies and needs for sexual gratification, but without giving a thought to his needs or the psychiatric issue(s) responsible for her unethical and pathological behavior. Perhaps, in most instances, this kind of sexual predator is harmless to most boys but, in some instances, it may create psychological damage for the rest of his life as it does with little girls.

Our history is full of such stories and some of them with a long continuity of psychological damage to the families.

There are instances of a man and woman, involved in a sexual relationship between each other, seeking out underage children for exploitation. The woman may find an underage woman, exploits her sexually for her sexual gratification within the fulfillment of her sexual fantasies with a woman and, then, when done with her, passes her on to her boyfriend for his sexual gratification with women.

One historical example would be the relationship between Jean-Paul Sartre (b. Jun 21, 1905; d. Apr. 15, 1980) and Simone de Beauvoir (b. Jan. 9, 1908; d. April 14, 1986).

Jean-Paul Sartre was a French philosopher, playwright, novelist, screenwriter, political activist, biographer, literary critic and an important person in the philosophy of Existentialism, as well as a leading figure in 20th century French philosophy and the ideology of Marxism.

Simone de Beauvoir was also a French writer, an intellectual personality, an Existential Philosopher, political activist, feminist and even a social theorist.

They held a life-long sexual relationship with each other. Jean-Paul Sartre may have been strictly heterosexual who entertained sexual fantasies with women; but Simone de Beauvoir clearly bisexual who entertained sexual fantasies with both men and women. She was a teacher in a secondary school who, apparently, judging from some accounts, routinely seduced some of her female students and then passed them on to her boyfriend, Jean-Paul Sartre. Both of them then shared each other's sexual fantasies with each other and with her female students.

Probably the most dangerous — indeed, evil — sexual fantasy is the sexual fantasy with children (*Pedophilia*). A pedophile can easily destroy an entire family over a period of several generations.

Pedophiles can be male or female, although most of American society — with the exception of the experts on the subject — tends to think all or most pedophiles to be middle-age adult men.

In truth, women can be just as abusive as any man on this subject can and both men and women can be of any age group. Women also have more exposure and opportunity with children than men and, for that reason alone, get away with it more often.

The problem is not the fantasy, per se, as most of us have that capability to make such a fantasy, but the implementation of the fantasy without a conscience. For a pedophile to fulfill his fantasy requires an interference with a child's life as he matures into adulthood. Such interference can easily lead to psychiatric damages as a direct result of this interference. These damages can even carry onto the next generation — and beyond.

It is outside the scope of this book to go into greater detail as long as we understand the inherent danger of receiving, or seeking out, sexual gratification with a child when motivated and driven by a sexual fantasy with a child. In this context, this kind of sexual fantasy is very dangerous.

Pedophilia, over the centuries, has had many definitions in psychiatry, psychology, law and, of course, in the colloquial speech. Indeed, it may not even been recognized as a mental disorder until the mid 19th century. Until then, there was no uniform recognition of it a being dangerous criminal behavior toward children. We have ancient manuscripts, such as *"Xenophon: Anabasis, the March up Country,"* an

Jean-Paul Sartre and Simone de Beauvoir

account of ancient warriors marching across country with the writer making a reference to a behavior we now recognize as *Pedophilia*. It took place around 431 BCE. In it, we will find a reference to one warrior's sexual orientation of preferring boys, or "*He who likes young boys with pretty faces.*" Though no recognition in this manuscript of it being a mental disorder, as such, the writer nevertheless thought of the warrior's behavior as a little unusual or, else, he will not have mentioned it. The warriors he knew were probably men who preferred women as sexual partners.

Generally speaking, *Pedophilia* refers to adult men or women who fantasize sex and receives sexual gratification with children under the age of 13.

*Ephebophilia* is the word to refer to adult men or women who fantasize sex and receives sexual gratification with children between the age of 15 and 19.

*Hebephilia* is the word to refer to adult men or women who fantasize sex and receives sexual gratification with children between the age of 11 and 14.

For the people who fantasize sex and receives sexual gratification with infants and toddlers, the word to describe such behavior is *Nepiophilia*.

### Abuses by Victims of Sexual Abuse —

All too often, there is a local guttersnipe, who uses the words Gay, Lesbian or Pedophile to describe people of whom he dislikes or misunderstands, such as the young boy or girl not yet dating or sexually active, or someone of whom he fears, envies or feels jealousy he converted into hate. Sniping can be just as dangerous and destructive as the real sexual abusers, and is not something we should tolerate.

There is also a pattern of people, when subject to sexual abuse as a child, to either suspect or consider all adult men or women as sexual abusers, depending on the sex of the abuser and the nature of the abuse.

Some victims will never entirely trust anyone after these experiences. Such experiences can easily cause a permanent and dangerous distortion in their interpretation of reality for them when unable to differentiate abusers from non-abusers.

We have instances of victims of sexual abuse calling the police or filing criminal charges against a man or woman for giving candy, ice cream or loose change to children out of kindness. For them, it is proof of pedophilia. Even taking a photograph of children in a church, county fair or circus is evidence of pedophilia by some victims. When the police conduct a routine investigation, as may be required by law, but finds no evidence of pedophilia, these victims may even so perceive it as proof of collusion with the police.

There is an incident in April of 2010 of a security officer, working in a large apartment complex in Springfield, Massachusetts, late one evening, who successfully stopped a 27-year old man from abducting and raping a little 10-year old. When he woke up the following morning, he found the report of capture and arrest of the perpetrator in the local newspapers and an article on internet describing him as a "hero" who saved the life of a little girl.

Then, over a period of several months, the story of his heroic efforts of saving a little girl's life was twisted. Now, instead of being the security officer who saved the life of a little girl, the gossip mill reversed the order to make him into the perpetrator who abducted and tried to rape a little 10-year old girl. Within a short succession, he found the local police department conducting a criminal investigation of him pursuant to a complaint from a resident of another apartment complex after seeing him patrolling the streets.

Another woman, a victim of sexual abuse as a child, continually called the police to demand another investigation. On several occasions, she called his boss to demand the security officer's discharge from employment. When unsuccessful, she personally went to the Property Manager's office to demand he refuse to allow the security officer to work in that complex consisting of dozens of children — in order "to protect the little children." It took an application for a criminal complaint in the local state district court against this woman to stop the criminal harassment against him. That process took several months to complete and, in the meanwhile, the security officer found it dangerous to work in that particular area. He was re-assigned elsewhere.

### The Power of Sexual Fantasy —

As we can appreciate, the use of sexual fantasy can be

pure pleasure or the source of great pain and damage to the personality or entire generations of a given family. What is remarkable about sexual fantasy is its power and versatility.

We can use fantasy to hurt someone in order to receive gratification; to fantasize making love during masturbation in order to relieve sexual tension or emotional stress; or to share a fantasy for mutual gratification with a partner. There are instances of a man and woman reversing their roles to enhance sexual pleasure. The man would play the part of a submissive and obedient woman entertaining a woman's sexual fantasy while the woman plays the part of the dominating male entertaining a man's sexual fantasy.

The only problem, as some women see it, is the man's power to immediately terminate this role at will and revert back to his original role. After all, he has the penis and the superior physical strength to dominate and control her. Still again, she can re-configure her fantasy to receive pleasure out of his dominance as he dominates her through control of the role they play as long as he does not abuse his power over her. Abuse will destroy her fantasy very quickly, though she may just as quickly configure another fantasy.

It is a powerful computer program that, if it works correctly, as Mother Nature intended it to work, can help a person to live a more successful and productive life. If it does not work correctly, then it can lead to pure hell for anyone with dysfunctional fantasy-making machinery due to errors in the DNA code written by Mother Nature.

Equally obvious, we have the power to emulate its power through the development of man-made technology. So, it is not a power beyond our ability to duplicate or to correct the DNA code written by Mother Nature. Eventually, once the science and technology becomes available in the future, we can develop the capability to duplicate it for our own original engineering applications. In time, when we understand it well enough, we may even rewrite part of the genetic code inside of us to correct defects and flaws written by Mother Nature.

Unique is the ability of sexual fantasy to allow both sides in a sexual relationship to receive gratification in either role — active or submissive. An important example is oral sex. The man, thinking of himself as in control of the relationship, enjoys the sheer pleasant of a woman performing oral sex on him. The woman, on the other hand, also thinks of herself as in control of the relationship and, in truth, as she looks at it, the only time she has any real power over him. He is defenseless to her and she knows it. He may not know it, however.

Truthfully, it is the woman who thinks she is in control over him during the act of oral sex, and the man who thinks he has the raw power to require she perform oral sex for him. This power relationship works in both directions at the same time, all due to the distinct characteristics of human sexual fantasy.

As is true with every attribute of power, it can lead to abuse without a balance in our application of power over each other. To be successful, there has to be a balance, and that is the man's responsibility, although the woman can help to provide direction for him with a little feminine tack and diplomacy. Even if they hurt each other, they will accept it as long they continue to be honest and correct their mistakes.

We can provide several examples. One of the most conspicuous examples of abuse is a man's requirement she perform oral sex on him without his reciprocating by performing oral sex on her, or something equally as powerful or as equivalent in its pleasure for her. Though she will continue to receive pleasure in the power of controlling him during oral sex, it will wear off in its depth as she begins to recognize his selfishness.

Still, this sexual act can lead to some interesting corollary effects and, sometimes, pathological situations. One interesting upshot of oral sex is the woman who develops an addiction to it. She does not require a reciprocating action from the man to continue gratification. All she requires is his cooperation. She will willingly do everything else. That means she will continue to perform long after he runs dry and then feels the frustration when he wants to sleep without the interruptions or the ability to turn over. Some such women enjoy the hot semen rushing down their throats and may even explode each time with an orgasm of their own, and others may find it an intermission and frustration every time he ejaculates. Some women find it repulsive and others thoroughly enjoy it. Some women incorporate oral sex in their sexual fantasies and others resolutely refuse to do so, thinking of it as dirty. Everyone is different in his needs but still common in the overall scheme of things.

Sometimes, though it may not cause any psychological or physical damage to the victim, it may represent some strange pathological conditions, nonetheless. One example would a housewife who just gave birth to a lovely boy. She is married to a man who works long hours leaving her alone in their house with a small infant. She enjoys sex with her husband but feels frustrated over his long absence every day. Lonely and unfulfilled, she spends long hours fantasizing making love to a man while masturbating.

Everything is alright until, one day; he comes home early to find his wife performing oral sex on their infant son.

## Cultural Influences over Interpretation of Pedophilia –

Over time, after we had completed a systematic investigation of this important subject of pedophilia, it became obvious culture has a most profound effect over everyone's interpretation of it.

In our present American culture, as well as many cultures throughout the world today, but not necessarily in the recent or distant past, there are automatic assumptions people who enjoy looking at children in the nude, or taking photographs of them in the nude, are pedophiles, meaning people who entertain a sexual fantasy of making love to children, or who exploit children for sexual pleasure or financial gain.

A study of this history will reveal this is not always the truth or even the proper interpretation of this phenomenon.

We have many historical instances of exceptions. One extremely important exception is Lewis Carroll, the pen name for Charles Lutwidge Dodgson (b. 27 Jan. 1832; d. 14 Jan. 1898).

Charles Lutwidge Dodgson (pen name,
Lewis Carroll), English Writer, Logician,
Mathematician, Anglican deacon, inventor
and Photographer [Public Domain image]

This man was responsible for no less than 13 literary works and 11 significant works on the science of mathematics, plus two unclassified pieces of work (source: Wikipedia, the free encyclopedia).

His literary work consisted mainly of what we call today, "Literary nonsense," in sharp contrast to his serious scientific works on mathematics.

"Literary nonsense" refers to a special kind of serious literature consisting of "layers" of nonsensical statements over layers   of nonsensical statements, such as in "Alice's Adventures in Wonderland," "Through the Looking-Glass," "The Hunting of the Snark" or "Jabberwocky." This kind of literature is meant to be for pure enjoyment and entertainment, and has no ulterior motives, agenda or hidden meanings in "between the lines." It is not philosophy, a prediction of the future or criticism of either the past or present.

Interestingly, as an amateur photographer, his expertise, or one of them, was the photography of naked children without any sexual connotations to them. He also took pictures of adult men, women, landscapes and animals. Pictures of naked children were taken with the explicit permission of their parents and, apparently, always with their parents present at his studio.

In the Victorian culture of the time, people perceived the nudity of a child as "an expression of innocence" – not as the subject of sexual abuse. During the time of Dodgson's life, child nudity was widespread and at the height of fashion without the sexual connotation we place upon it today. Even Christmas cards, not uncommonly, contained photographs of naked children, clearly demonstrating a diverse social and artistic representation of the beauty of the human body in a totally different cultural outlook.

Many years after his death, without taking the time to study the differences in culture between his past and their present, and with an enormous change in their cultures since then, many critics interpreted his photography of naked children as evidence of pedophilia. Not until many, many years later, when more biographical data became available for a closer examination of this man, did historians finally recognize his photography of naked children as a representation of the prevalent folkways and mores of his culture as well as a genuine artistic expression of childhood beauty.

\*\*\*

# Chapter Nine

## *A Synopsis or Summation*

### Introduction —

As we ought to recognize by now, the subject of human sexual fantasy and sexual orientation is enormously complex with almost an endless assortment of offshoots and repercussions throughout human history. Hence, I have made no attempt to cover every single possibility on this critically important subject.

Frankly, I do not have enough experience to do so. To complicate matters, most people do not ordinarily openly discuss their sexual fantasies in the public, for this reason making it nearly impossible for anyone to perceive and recognize the cause and effect relationships — least of all to study it scientifically. We do know, however, the sexual fantasy we use determines our sexual orientation. We also know enough to recognize sexual fantasy as an essential mechanism for each of us, as living human beings in our reproductive endeavors, as well as a dangerous weapon when we use it incorrectly. We know enough to realize people using the wrong sexual fantasy for his sex and gender, with some exceptions and without understanding any of it, lives a life of turmoil, stress, frustration and disappointment.

A person with a man's body and a man's brain who uses or entertains a sexual fantasy with women and a person with a woman's body and a woman's brain who uses or entertains a sexual fantasy with men — are heterosexual.

On the other hand, a person with a man's body and a man's brain who uses or entertains a sexual fantasy with men and a person with a woman's body and a woman's brain who uses or entertains a sexual fantasy with women — are homosexual.

We know there are some people who use or entertain sexual fantasies with both men and women, and call it bisexuality.

History has revealed some people use sexual fantasies with animals, and some of them will revert back and forth between men, women and animals to suit their needs in an enhancement or intensification of their orgasms during either sex or masturbation. We call this phenomenon Zoophilia or Bestiality.

We have also learned there are at least 20 different sexual orientations or variations outside of the normal heterosexual orientation. Some of these sexual orientations are dangerous. Others are harmless though a little bizarre.

## Problems Defining Dysfunctional Sexual Orientation as a Mental Disorder —

We have discovered psychiatry cannot handle this subject due to its controversiality as it struggles for a definitive definition of mental disorder, particularly a definitive definition of homosexuality and other sexual orientations.

The homosexual community has intimidated psychiatry since late 1979, forcing the American Psychiatric Association to work around it using meaningless abstractions and technical jargon. While the Community resolutely refuses to accept its sexual orientation as a mental disorder, other than normalcy, they prove consistently unable to provide their own definitive definition American psychiatry can accept. Obviously, they do not know any more about the cause and effect relationships of their dysfunctional sexual orientation than anyone else. They hold the same ignorance, if not more so. All we have to do is to read their literature to expose their ignorance and witness the display of an air of superiority to conceal or mask their inferiority complex.

In the DSM-IV edition, published in 1994, as stated earlier, a mental disorder, before we can list anything as a mental disorder, must demonstrate a *"clinically significant distress or impairment in social, occupational, or other important areas of functioning."*

That kind of definition would represent a person's reaction to the recognition of his problem, after comparing himself to the heterosexual community, not a study or analysis of the cause of his problem. We do not have the science to answer that question, just a lot of theory, religious rationalizations, silly nonsense with vulgarisms and Junk Science.

On the surface, it would be difficult for us to argue with the above definition. When we go into significant detail, however, it begins to break down. A person can have a sexual orientation nowhere near that of a correct heterosexual orientation and, still, function perfectly normally without any stress or impairment. Indeed, he may not even be aware of his problem. So that definition is inadequate due to a lack of a real knowledge of the cause and effect relationships of his incorrect use of a sexual fantasy.

An example would be a person with a sexual orientation of implementing a sexual fantasy with small children. He may not experience *"significant distress or impairment in social, occupational, or other important areas of functioning."* To the average person, perhaps someone who has not studied the subject, he may appear perfectly normal with no hint of an abnormal sexual orientation. That happens all of the time. Not until he rapes a little boy or girl and law enforcement catches him, does he reveal his true sexual orientation. Then that creates a catastrophic repercussion for at least two families, his family and the victim's family, sometimes for several generations for both families.

In an earlier edition of DSM, the DSM-III, published in 1980, the Task Force at the time replaced *"sexual orientation disturbance,"* originating in the 1974 edition of DSM-II, with the diagnostic definition of homosexuality as an *"ego-dystonic sexual orientation"* or an *"ego-dystonic mental disorder,"* characterized as *"having a sexual orientation or an attraction that is at odds with one's idealized self-image, causing anxiety and a desire to change one's orientation or become more comfortable with one's sexual orientation."*

Again, there is that problem. It fails to address the cause and effect relationships! It fails to describe dysfunctional sexual orientations, or to explain the cause of some people using the wrong sexual fantasy for his sex and gender. Nor can it provide any measure of treatment. Without understanding the cause of the condition, we cannot treat it.

## The Difference between Sex and Gender —

Sex refers to the sex of the body and its sexual components. If it has a scrotum and penis, then the body is male and, if not, but a labia, clitoris and vagina, then a female.

Gender, on the other hand, refers to what the brains thinks of itself. If the brain thinks of itself as a man, then it is a man and, if a woman, then it is a woman. The brain is always right.

If a person is born with a man's body and a man's brain, who uses or entertains a sexual fantasy with women, then that is normal for our species. As he grows up and matures into an adult, he will learn to appreciate his gender and sex and think of it as advantageous over a woman with his power to define and control the relationship with her, using his power over her as an integral part of his sexual fantasies.

If a person is born with a woman's body and a woman's brain, who uses or entertains a sexual fantasy with men, then that is normal for our species. As she grows up and matures into a woman, she will perceive his power to define and control the relationship with her as well as her power to modulate the power he has over her. She is not overly upset with his power, as long as he does not abuse it, and may indeed use his power as an integral part of her sexual fantasies. That is normal for her with a heterosexual orientation.

It is normal for him to enjoy his power over her and normal for her to enjoy her power to modulate his power, an integral part of our total genetic program in the DNA, the genetic code responsible for the makeup of our physical and some of our psychological characteristics.

However, there are many exceptions. Some boys grow up into men jealous of women with their power, the ability to use their physical and sexual attractiveness to control men and the power to give birth to children. Nor are women expected to work for a living. They have a common-law traditional right to expect man to support them while they stay home to give birth to children and to raise them into adulthood.

Some men grow up jealous of a woman's right to stay home while the man works. They would prefer to stay home while the woman works.

Some girls grow up into women jealous of man's power to control the relationship with them, without recognizing their corresponding power, and some of them prefer to work while he stays home. Some women, particularly the Lesbian community, would prefer to possess both powers, unable to relate with the heterosexual orientation between a man and woman. They see the relationship as abusive or inappropriate to their needs.

Some women do not desire to give birth to children, but prefer to give that responsibility and power to a man, or at least to allow other women to do it. On the other hand, most women thoroughly enjoy that power to bear children, and it is no secret women also thoroughly enjoy that power over a man. It is a power no man can possess. Only a woman can bear children. So, in that respect, they think of themselves as superior to man although, at the same time, jealous of him.

There is also another role each of us plays in a heterosexual relationship. Usually, the man plays the active role and the woman the passive role and, as strange as it sounds, due to the nature of the power relationship between man and woman, both of them are equal to each other even when she is subservient to him or playing the role of a love-slave. We have many historical instances of a woman intellectually superior to her husband, or in a financially superior position, playing the subservient role — and both of them perfectly comfortable with it. Subservience does not mean inferiority!

## Exceptions Outside of the Heterosexual Orientation —

We realize the correct sexual orientation for our species is that of a sexual fantasy with members of the opposite sex. A man fantasizes sex with a woman and a woman fantasizes sex with a man. Most of us have an inherent capability to expand our fantasies to arouse each other and ourselves without using them outside of a heterosexual relationship. That is normal and part of our genetic code. Only when there is no capability to fantasize sex with a member of the opposite sex do we have a problem. For a fantasy of sex with the opposite sex is absolutely imperative for a normal heterosexual relationship.

We also realize not every person is born with this sexual orientation. Some people are born with the capability to use sexual fantasy with only members of the opposite sex and others use fantasies of sex with members of the same sex, both sexes or with animals. Some people do not use a sexual fantasy of any kind; still, some of them manage to emulate a normal heterosexual relationship with the opposite sex by watching and studying the behavior of other people. Some people have the capability to switch their gender to suit their moods for the day and others find their gender switching back and forth randomly without control or the power to shut it down.

We do not know the reason for these inconsistencies, other than reasoning it as an error in the genetic code. It leaves such people in a constant state of confusion and creates enormous problems of adjustment to their environment and, in some environments, makes it even dangerous for them.

Unlike a heterosexual relationship between a man and woman, the power relationship between two men or two women, in a homosexual relationship, is not the same. Though they can adopt children, they cannot produce children between themselves. They can make love among themselves and thoroughly enjoy sex; nevertheless, it is not the same power relationship as it is between a man and a woman. It is just a form of mutual masturbation motivated and driven by the wrong sexual fantasy.

### Recognition of a Need for a Scientific Study of Sexual Orientations —

From all accounts, it has grown increasingly obvious this variation of our sexual fantasies from person to person, which determines our sexual orientation, has been with us since the inception of our species. It is not something new that popped into our consciousness a few years ago. We can find references of different sexual orientations in world literature going back more than 2,500 years ago and rock engravings nearly 40,000 years ago.

We have historical evidence medical science has been studying the human body for several thousand years. In ancient Rome, medical wisdom lost during the Middle-Ages, there was a remarkable capability to repair the human body with primitive instruments and limited knowledge of the internal functions of the human body, though admittedly, most of it originally designed to repair our bodies damaged from combat between men.

For less than 200 years, there has been a serious scientific study of the human brain. Not until the development of sophisticated instruments in the last few years, such as X-Ray, Ultrasound, CAT-Scan, MRI or the Computed Tomography (CT) Scan, did we really learn anything.

Yet, in spite of these enormous accomplishments, with some of our knowledge lost over time and then re-learned, we have never taken the time to study, on a legitimate scientific level, the effect of human sexual fantasy over our sexual orientation. Simply reading some of our world literature will reveal a huge variation in the interpretation of sexual orientation, some of it interesting but most of it sheer nonsense or pure fraud. Combined or separate, none of it adds up to a real knowledge, or to a useable scientific database, unlike the science databases for cancer or diabetes. We cannot look it up in a medical or psychiatric dictionary for treatment, either. Such dictionaries do not exit. Part of this reason is self-evident. This subject is unbelievably complicated. Another, more important reason is our culture. We do not have the freedom to openly discuss and analyze human sexuality, thus making it difficult for anyone to think it out. If we cannot think about it, then we cannot analyze it and, without analyzing it, we can never understand it. Sex is not dirty. It is just another subject we need to study and understand.

The closest thing to this subject is pornography, and that only applies to some parts of the world with a freedom of speech. Anyone who attempts to discuss sex without vulgarisms or pornographic images will run into problems with almost everyone. Some people will pretend to be indignant and others will simply shut off their brains while pretending the subject to be dirty. In truth, they cannot handle it. They rationalize their ignorance with pretences of indignation to mask their ignorance.

Pornography is, of course, an important subject and, contrary to conventional wisdom, important for people who need to know at least something about sex, other than what they will have learned from the Grapevines. We use pornography to teach us about our bodies and, frankly, it provides the programming code for the use of fantasy during masturbation.

Pornography enhances or augments fantasy through a clarification of the physical details and allows us to see the variations in shapes, sizes and colors of human male and female bodies — all of it important to everyone. No exception!

Psychiatry has failed in its responsibility to study the subject scientifically. Another conspicuous failure is the failure to define mental disorder. Although most of us can easily recognize a mentally ill person, or think we can do most of the time, it is far more difficult to define it. Also, far too many people are quick to assess a person as being mentally ill when, in truth, he is simply a little different from the norm. We can deviate significantly from the norm without being mentally ill, an attribute within each of us too many people cannot readily understand or appreciate. We are not robots or clones. Though all of us have the same machinery inside of us, save for sex and gender, each of us is a little different from each other. That is what differentiates us from robots and clones. We are humans.

In addition, as reported in Chapter One, each of us has millions of components inside each of us, any of which can go bad. We are a very, very complex machine; in spite of the fact we have been studying the subject for thousands of years, we still understand very little about ourselves. While each of us has these millions of components, the most complex component is not even physical. That non-physical component is a computer program with its application software package serving as an engine driving our sexual orientation. Indeed, it is so complex; most of us do not even perceive its existence or purpose.

True, most of us can perceive our use of a sexual fantasy, and consciously use it extensively, but fail to recognize it as a non-physical machine responsible for our sexual orientation. It also appears obvious there is a genetic code inside each of us responsible for it and it occasionally comes out written incorrectly, probably before birth. Some of this code can be damaged through sexual abuse during our critical formative years of development (see page 108).

In full view of its significance to human reality, we would think — not just psychiatry — but the entire medical field would spend much more time studying it.

Until we can understand it more fully, identify the exact DNA code responsible for our sexual orientation and develop the science and technology to correct the errors, this world mental health crisis will continue.

\*\*\*

# A Special Note of Interest

In October 7, 2012, I was writing an e-mail message to a literary agent in the state of Utah about a manuscript I am working on presently. I said it was on a highly controversial subject entitled, "The Power of Human Sexual Fantasy, Its Effect over Human Development, Culture, Crime and Relationships." (I changed the title since then) I remember telling her sexual fantasy is a computer program. Its primary application is that of a navigational system with powerful motivational and driving attributes, the mechanism that determines our sexual orientation. If we were to write out our own computer program to emulate sexual fantasy, I said, we would create significant engineering applications that could lead to the development of new industries.

Then, I went into some detail explaining I am looking for a publisher to handle it. I will send the first chapter to her in the form of an "attachment" in the Microsoft Office Word document 2007 format (.docx), I told her.

Interestingly, after I had completed my text, I absentmindedly placed the mouse cursor over the word "Send" to send the message forgetting to include the attachment when, to my surprise, a small dialog box popped up on the screen.

It said, "Did you forget to include your attachment?"

Though admittedly not an expert in this area of computer science, I have enough knowledge to understand this primitive text processor in Hotmail's e-mail provider does not have the artificial intelligence algorithms to read my text in real-time, to draw an interpretation or to respond to it. That capability took a 3rd party illegally monitoring my w on the computer.

I do not know who did it. It could have been a hacker positively bored out of his mind when the subject matter (sexual fantasy) caught his attention. When I failed to include the attachment, he foolishly revealed his presence with that dialog box.

Of course, we cannot discount the possibility of an American federal agency, such as the National Security Agency, or a foreign government, such as China, Russia, North Korea, Iran, etc. All of them employ hackers, including the NSA, a recent revelation in the World Press.

Then, a few months later, I began to realize someone was turning on my GPS (Global Position System) in my cell phone. Sometimes, the battery would run dry within five to seven hours when, normally, it would last more than a whole week. I would re-charge the battery and shut off the GPS.

Within a few hours, someone or something would turn it back on again. Unable to control my own cell phone, I shut off the cell phone, closed my account with Virgin Wireless, and then purchased a new cell phone without the GPS feature.

Shortly after this decision, I read an account in the local newspaper and news articles on internet reporting the NSA may have been responsible for this criminal activity.

***

# Bibliography

Adam, Barry (1987). "The Rise of a Gay and Lesbian Movement", G.      K. Hall & Co. ISBN 0-8057-9714-9

Aldrich, Robert, ed. (2006). "Gay Life and Culture: A World History", Thames & Hudson, Ltd. ISBN 0-7893-1511-4

Aylwin, A. Scott; Reddon, John R.; Burke, Andrew R. (2005), "Sexual Fantasies of Adolescent Male Sex Offenders in Residential Treatment: A Descriptive Study", Archives of Sexual Behavior 34 (2): 231–239, doi:10.1007/s10508-005-1800-3, PMID 15803256

Bagemihl, Bruce (1999), "Biological Exuberance: Animal Homosexuality and Natural Diversity", St. Martin's Press, ISBN 0-312-19239-8

Bernstein, Elizabeth; Schaffner, Laurie (2005), "Regulating sex: the politics of intimacy and identity", Routledge, ISBN 978-0-415-94869-2

Bérubé, Allan, "Coming out under Fire: The History of Gay Men and Women in World War Two", New York: MacMillan 1990, ISBN 0-02-903100-1

Bhugra, Dinesh; Rahman, Qazi; Bhintade, Rahul (2006), "Sexual fantasy in gay men in India: a comparison with heterosexual mean", Sexual and Relationship Therapy 21 (2): 197–207, doi:10.1080/14681990600554207

Birnbaum, Gurit E. (2007), "Beyond the borders of reality: Attachment orientations and sexual fantasies", Personal Relationships 14 (2): 321–342, 10.1111/j.1475-6811.2007.00157.x

Boswell, John (1980), "Christianity, Social Tolerance, and Homosexuality: Gay People in Western Europe from the Beginning of the Christian Era to the Fourteenth Century", University of Chicago Press, ISBN 978-0-226-06711-7

Bremmer, Jan (ed.) (1989). "From Sappho to de Sade: Moments in the History of Sexuality", Routledge. ISBN 0-415-02089-1

Brenshoff, Harry, Griffin, Sean (2006). "Queer Images: A History of Gay and Lesbian Film in America", Rowman & Littlefield Publishers, Inc. ISBN 0-7425-1971-6

Brown, Lester B. (1997), Lester B. Brown, ed., "Two spirit people: American Indian, lesbian women and gay men", Routledge, ISBN 978-0-7890-0003-3

Bullough, Vern L.; Brundage, James A. (2000), "Handbook of medieval sexuality", Taylor & Francis, ISBN 978-0-8153-3662-4

Bullough, Vern L. (2002), "Before Stonewall: activists for gay and lesbian rights in historical context", Routledge, ISBN 978-1-56023-193-6

Carlson, Earl R.; Coleman, Catherine Elaine Havelock (1977), "Experiential and motivational determinants of the richness of an induced sexual fantasy", Journal of Personality 45 (4): 528–542, doi:10.1111/j.1467-6494.1977.tb00169.x, PMID 592084

Castle, Terry, ed. (2003). "The Literature of Lesbianism: A Historical Anthology from Ariosto to Stonewall", Columbia University Press. ISBN 0-231-12510-0

Chauncey, George (1995), "Gay New York: Gender, Urban Culture, and the Making of the Gay Male World, 1890–1940" (reprint, illustrated ed.), Basic Books, ISBN 978-0-465-02621-0 d'Emilio, John, "Sexual Politics, Sexual Communities: The Making of a Homosexual Minority in the United States, 1940–1970", University of Chicago Press 1983, ISBN 0-226-14265-5

Davidson, James (2007). "The Greeks and Greek Love: A Radical Reappraisal of Homosexuality in Ancient Greece". Weidenfeld & Nicolson. ISBN 0-297-81997-6.

Doan, Laura (2001). "Fashioning Sapphism: The Origins of a Modern English Lesbian Culture", Columbia University Press. ISBN 0-231-11007-3

Dover, Kenneth J., "Greek Homosexuality", Gerald Duckworth & Co. Ltd. 1979, ISBN 0-674-36261-6 (hardcover), ISBN 0-674-36270-5 (paperback)

Dynes, Wayne R.; Johansson, Warren; Percy, William A.; Donaldson, Stephen (1990), "Encyclopedia of homosexuality (2 Volumes)", Garland Pub., ISBN 978-0-8240-6544-7

Edsall, Nicholas (2003). "Toward Stonewall: Homosexuality and Society in the Modern Western World", University of Virginia Press. ISBN 0-8139-2211-9

Ellis, Bruce J.; Symons, Donald (1990), "Sex Differences in Sexual Fantasy: an Evolutionary Psychological Approach", The Journal of Sex Research 27 (4): 527–555, doi:10.1080/00224499009551579, JSTOR 3812772

Faderman, Lillian (1981). "Surpassing the Love of Men: Romantic Friendship and Love Between Women from the Renaissance to the Present", Quill. ISBN 0-688-00396-6

Faderman, Lillian (1991). "Odd Girls and Twilight Lovers: A History of Lesbian Life in Twentieth Century America", Penguin Books. ISBN 0-14-017122-3

Faderman, Lillian (1993), "Odd girls and twilight lovers: a history of lesbian life in twentieth-century America" (4 ed.), Columbia University Press, ISBN 978-0-231-07488-9

Fisher, Seymour (1989), "Sexual Images of the Self: The Psychology of Erotic Sensations and Illusions" (First ed.), Hillsdale, New Jersey: Lawrence Erlbaum Associates, Inc., ISBN 978-0-8058-0439-3

Foster, Jeannette H. (1956). "Sex Variant Women in Literature", Naiad Press edition, 1985. ISBN 0-930044-65-7

Foucault, Michel (1986), "The History of Sexuality", Pantheon Books, ISBN 0-394-41775-5

Gallo, Marcia (2006). "Different Daughters: A History of the Daughters of Bilitis and the Rise of the Lesbian Rights Movement", Seal Press. ISBN 1-58005-252-5

Hamer, Diane, Budge, Belinda, eds. (1994). "The Good, The Bad, and the Gorgeous: Popular Culture's Romance with Lesbianism", Pandora. ISBN 0-04-440910-9

Heiman, Julia R. (1977), "A Psychophysiological Exploration of Sexual Arousal Patterns in Females and Males", Psychophysiology 14 (3): 266–274, doi:10.1111/j.1469-8986.1977.tb01173.x, PMID 854556

Hinsch, Bret, "Passions of the Cut Sleeve: The Male Homosexual Tradition in China", the University of California Press, 1990, ISBN 0-520-06720-7

Holmes, King, Sparling, P., et al., eds. (2008). "Sexually Transmitted Diseases", McGraw-Hill Medical. ISBN 0-07-141748-6

Jeffrey, Robinson. "What is Context Specific Therapy?". Self-published. Retrieved 2007-10-29.

Jennings, Rebecca (2007). "A Lesbian History of Britain", Greenwood World Publishing. ISBN 1-84645-007-1

Johansson, Warren; William A. Percy (1994), "Outing: shattering the conspiracy of silence", Routledge, ISBN 978-1-56024-419-6

Johnson, David K. (2004), "The lavender scare: the Cold War persecution of gays and lesbians in the federal government", University of Chicago Press, ISBN 978-0-226-40481-3

Katz, Jonathan (1976). "Gay American History: Lesbians and Gay Men in the U.S.A" Thomas Y. Crowell Company. ISBN 0-690-01165-2

Kleinplatz, Peggy J. (2001). "New directions in sex therapy: innovations and alternatives." Psychology Press. p. 100. ISBN 978-0-87630-967-4.

Knox, Jean (2005), "Sex, shame and the transcendent function: the function of fantasy in self development", Journal of Analytical Psychology 50 (5): 617–639, doi:10.1111/j.0021-8774.2005.00561.x, PMID 16255728

Leitenberg, Harold; Henning, Kris (1995), "Sexual Fantasy", Psychological Bulletin 117 (3): 469–496, doi:10.1037/0033-2909.117.3.469, PMID 7777650

McCormick, Noami (1994). "Sexual Salvation: Affirming Women's Sexual Rights and Pleasures", Praeger Publishers. ISBN 0-275-94359-3

Mednick, Robert A. (1977), "Gender-Specific Variances in Sexual Fantasy", Journal of Personality Assessment 41 (3): 248–254, doi:10.1207/s15327752jpa4103_4, PMID 886421

Michael, Robert T. (1994), "Sex in America: a definitive survey", Little, Brown, ISBN 978-0-316-91191-7

Murray, Stephen O. and Roscoe, Will (1997). "Islamic Homosexualities: Culture, History and Literature", New York University Press. ISBN 0-8147-7468-7

"NARTH 2003 Annual Conference schedule". NARTH. 2004-04-14. Archived from the original on November 15, 2006. Retrieved 2007-10-29.

Nicholas, L.J. (2004), "The Association between Religiosity, Sexual Fantasy, Participation in Sexual Acts, Sexual Enjoyment, Exposure, and Reaction to Sexual Materials Among Black South Africans", Journal of Sex & Marital Therapy 30 (1): 37–42, doi:10.1080/00926230490247264

Norton, Rictor (1997). "The Myth of the Modern Homosexual: Queer History and the Search for Cultural Unity", Cassell. ISBN 0-304-33892-3

Percy, William Armstrong (1998), "Pederasty and Pedagogy in Archaic Greece", University of Illinois Press, ISBN 978-0-252-06740-2

Rabinowitz, Nancy, Auanger, Lisa, eds. (2002). "Among Women: From the Homosocial to the Homoerotic in the Ancient World", University of Texas Press. ISBN 0-292-77113-4

Rachid, María (2000). "Encuentros de lesbianas". In George Haggerty & Bonnie Zimmerman (Eds.), Encyclopedia of Lesbians and gay histories and cultures. Taylor & Francis. ISBN 978-0-8153-1920-7

Rathus, Spencer A.; Nevid, Jeffrey S.; Fichner-Rathus, Lois; Herold, Edward S.; McKenzie, Sue Wicks (2005), "Human sexuality in a world of diversity" (Second ed.), New Jersey, USA: Pearson Education, ISBN 978-0-205-40615-9

Rothblum, Esther, Brehoney, Kathleen, eds. (1993). "Boston Marriages: Romantic but Asexual Relationships among Contemporary Lesbians", University of Massachusetts Press. ISBN 0-87023-875-2

Russo, Vito (1987). "The Celluloid Closet: Homosexuality in the Movies", Harper & Row. ISBN 0-06-096132-5

Schmitt, Arno; Jehoeda Sofer (1992), Arno Schmitt; Jehoeda Sofer, eds., "Sexuality and eroticism among males in oslem societies", Routledge, ISBN 978-1-56024-047-1

Scott, Gunther. "The Elastic Closet: A History of Homosexuality in France, 1942–present" Book about the history of homosexual movements in France (sample chapter available online). New York: Palgrave-Macmillan, 2009. ISBN 0-230-22105-X.

Scott, Gini Graham (1994), "The Power of Fantasy: Illusion and Eroticism in Everyday Life" (First ed.), New York, New York: Carol Publishing Group, ISBN 978-1-55972-239-1

Smith, David; Over, Ray (1987), "Male Sexual Arousal as a Function of the Content and the Vividness of Erotic Fantasy", Psychophysiology 24 (3): 334–339, doi:10.1111/j.1469-8986.1987.tb00304.x, PMID 3602290

Strassberg, Donald S.; Lockerd, Lisa K. (August 1998), "Force in Women's Sexual Fantasies", Archives of Sexual Behavior 27 (4): 403–415, doi:10.1023/A:1018740210472, ISSN 1573-2800

Stryker, Susan (2001). "Queer Pulp: Perverted Passions from the Golden Age of the Paperback", Chronicle Books, LLC. ISBN 0-8118-3020-9

Sullivan, Gerard, Jackson, Peter, eds. (2001). "Gay and Lesbian Asia: Culture, Identity, Community", Harrington Park Press. ISBN 1-56023-146-7

Tamagne, Florence (2004). "A History of Homosexuality in Europe Berlin, London, Paris, 1919–1939: Volume 1", Algora. ISBN 0-585-49198-4

Terry, Jennifer (1999), "An American obsession: science, medicine, and homosexuality in modern society", University of Chicago Press, ISBN 978-0-226-79367-2

Throckmorton, Warren (2004). "What is reparative therapy?" Self-published. Retrieved 2007-10-29.

Tropiano, Stephen (2002). "Prime Time Closet: A History of Gays and Lesbians on TV", Applause Theater and Cinema Books. ISBN 1-55783-557-8

Vanita, Ruth (2002), "Queering India: same-sex love and eroticism in Indian culture and society", Routledge, ISBN 978-0-415-92950-9

Verstraete, Beert; Provencal, Vernon (eds.) (2005). "Same-Sex Desire and Love in Greco-Roman Antiquity and In the Classical Tradition of the West", Harrington Park Press. ISBN 1-56023-604-3

Warner, Tom (2002). "Never Going Back: A History of Queer Activism in Canada", University of Toronto Press. ISBN 0-8020-8460-5

Willett, Graham (2000). "Living Out Loud: A History of Gay and Lesbian Activism in Australia", Allen & Unwin. ISBN 1-74115-113-9

Wilson, Glenn Daniel (1978), "The secrets of sexual fantasy" (First ed.), London, England: J.M. Dent & Sons Ltd., ISBN 978-0-460-04309-0

Zimet, Jaye (1999). "Strange Sisters: The Art of Lesbian Pulp Fiction, 1949–1969", Viking Studio. ISBN 0-14-028402-8

Zimmerman (Eds.), Encyclopedia of lesbian and gay histories and cultures. Taylor & Francis. ISBN 978-0-8153-1920-7

Zimmerman, Bonnie, Ed (2003). "Lesbian Histories and Cultures: An Encyclopedia", Garland Publishers. ISBN 0-203-48788-5 1980s

# INDEX